101 EVERYDAY SAYINGS FROM THE BIBLE

By Ed Forster

CREST BOOKS

Salvation Army National Publications
615 Slaters Lane
Alexandria, Virginia 22313

Copyright © 2008 by The Salvation Army

Published by Crest Books
The Salvation Army National Headquarters
615 Slaters Lane, Alexandria, VA 22313
Major Ed Forster, Editor-in-Chief and National Literary Secretary
Major Christine Poff, Assistant to the Editor-in-Chief
Judith L. Brown, Crest Books Coordinator
Lisa Jones, Cover and Interior Design

Phone: 703/684-5523
Fax 703/302-8617

Available from The Salvation Army Supplies and Purchasing Departments
 Des Plaines, IL – (847) 937-8896
 West Nyack, NY – (888) 488-4882
 Atlanta, GA – (800) 786-7372
 Long Beach, CA – (847) 937-8896

Printed in the United States of America

We have chosen to upper case references to the Deity and related words for clarification and consistency.

Library of Congress Control Number: 2008932753
ISBN–13: 978-0-9792266-3-2

To my father and mother –
who, most of all,
loved us.

$\boxed{I}$ntroduction

My father was a fruit peddler in Boston. His family had come to the U.S. from Scotland. They used many colorful expressions that fascinated me as a boy. Once when I was working on my father's fruit truck, it was raining heavily and we had to stop working. On the way home, my dad said, "Well, we're not stopping because we want to, it's an act of God."

The use of such an expression made rain seem larger than life. My father made little things seem big because of his phrases. He had a host of names for money. He called a five-dollar bill a "finef." A "sawbuck" meant ten dollars, while a "double sawbuck" was twenty. When it got to a hundred, it was a "C–note," and a thousand was a "G."

Language fascinated me. Soon I began to hear expressions like, "a little birdie told me," and "the shoe is on the other foot." These word pictures stayed in my head and they delighted me.

While serving as pastor to a challenging congregation in Kearny, N.J., during the late 1970's, the light of connection dawned on me. I was listening to the Bible on cassette tapes in my car, trying to keep up with the heavy demands of sermon preparation. The narrator was reading from the Old Testament book of Ecclesiastes. Solomon's advice in the tenth chapter grabbed my ear. "Curse not the king, no not in thy thought; and curse not the rich in thy bedchamber: for a bird of the air shall carry the voice, and that which hath wings shall tell the matter" (vs. 20).

It hit me. "A little birdie told me," was in the Bible. I quickly rolled back the cassette to try and catch the phrase again. But the tape went too far back and landed on the first verse. "Dead flies cause the ointment of the apothecary to send forth a stinking savour," it said. "A fly in the ointment," my mind recalled. I asked myself, "Am I really hearing these expressions coming from the Bible?"

That event pushed me into research. The flavor and texture of sayings I'd been hearing all of my life came alive. I began sharing my discoveries from the pulpit. Later, it led to a series of speaking engagements outside of my congregation and then to magazine articles in The Salvation Army's national magazine, the *War Cry*.

People encouraged me to consider writing a book on the subject. With the help of a team of senior citizens in Pittsburgh, the project took shape. Their excitement reinforced the enthusiasm the sayings had received in a host of oral presentations. These phrases appealed to a wide variety of diverse age groups.

We discovered many things during our long hours poring over the scriptures. Here are some of the things we learned:

Our language is always changing. Words and phrases enter and leave it almost daily. Some parts of our English language, however, have staying power. There are some expressions that have been around for hundreds of years.

One of the principle sources of these commonly used expressions is the Bible, particularly the King James Version (KJV), first published in 1611. It has helped give these expressions stability.

The Bible has been the perennial best seller for years. There's at least one in almost every home in America, in hotel and motel rooms, libraries and churches. It is quoted from pulpits and lecterns regularly, but it is often quoted unknowingly in conversation.

Many people are surprised to discover how many times they use expressions from the Scriptures. References from the Bible have so woven themselves into our oral and written communication that we use them without thinking about their origin.

The Word of God is a powerful influence in daily life. It forms a foundation for government, provides plots for drama, inspires many art masterpieces and penetrates language even when we are not aware of it.

May you find as much pleasure reading about these expressions as I have had researching them, and discovering anew the wonderful influence of the Bible on our daily lives.

– Ed Forster

Contents

Adam's Apple

F ruit grew in abundance in the Garden of Eden. Most people contend that the fruit that grew on the tree of The Knowledge of Good and Evil, as described in Genesis, was an apple. In fact, no specific fruit is mentioned for this tree in the Bible.

Since our mouths and throats become dry when we are seized with guilt, many people have suggested that Adam choked on a piece of the "stolen fruit" when God questioned him about it. The assumption that the fruit was an apple has also led to the term Adam's Apple to describe the lump in the center of a man's neck.

Adam, in Genesis 3:10, admits he was afraid. "I heard thy voice in the garden, and I was afraid because I was naked; so I hid myself."

His fear caused him to hide from God. He also admitted to eating the fruit that he wasn't supposed to eat, but he blamed "The woman whom thou gavest to be with me" (3:12) for his actions.

No wonder ancient people believed the fruit got stuck in his throat. Adam had the audacity to say that the wrongdoing wasn't his fault, but Eve's, and more significantly, God's. He seemed to blame God for the eventual outcome of his own disobedience – that would make a piece of fruit stick in anyone's throat. It would even seem powerful enough to cause succeeding generations to inherit the trait.

The lump doesn't protrude very much in a woman's throat. Eve somehow escaped it, even though she inherited mankind's sinful nature along with Adam. One sage said, "It wasn't the apple on the tree that caused the sin – it was the 'pair' on the ground."

All Decked Out

O ne way to describe someone who dresses in fancy clothes and wears lots of jewelry is to say they are "all decked out." Our first impression might be to think that such a term originated in the navy, where ship decks are sometimes decorated for special occasions.

It was the minor prophet Hosea who used the term "decked" to describe the way the children of Israel adorned themselves while practicing idol worship. God detested their lack of spiritual values. He saw their behavior as spiritual prostitution against Him. He sent Hosea to speak against it.

Hosea was commanded by God to marry a prostitute who would be unfaithful to him. By his continual faithfulness to an unfaithful wife, Hosea displayed the kind of love that God had for His people who were unfaithful to Him through their idolatry.

The prophet, in carrying God's message against the nation of Israel, writes, "And I (God) will visit upon her (Israel) the days of Baalim, wherein she burned incense to them, and she decked herself with her earrings and her jewels, and she went after her lovers and forgat Me, saith the Lord" (Hosea 2:13).

Despite Israel's "decked out" behavior, God sought reconciliation by having Hosea continually call on Israel to change.

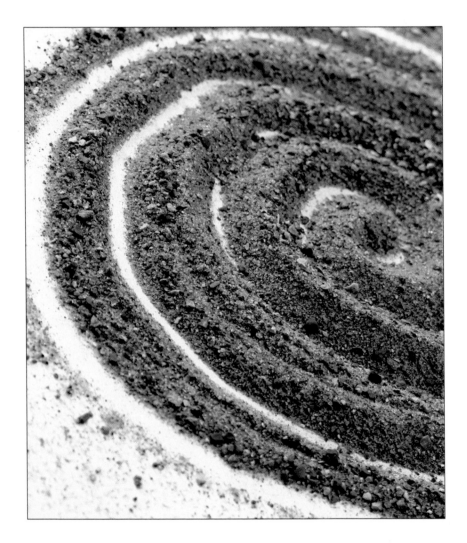

Alpha and Omega

A lpha is the beginning and omega is the end. This expression, "the alpha and omega" means the first and the last. Appropriately, they are the first and last letters in the Greek alphabet. We have a parallel expression in English, "from A to Z."

The phrase "alpha and omega" comes from the last book of the Bible, the Revelation of Saint John. We usually refer to the book as The Revelation.

Its author, John, the beloved disciple of Jesus, is the only one of the original 12 disciples who died of natural causes, according to church history. He lived a long life, spending the last portion of it banished to the Isle of Patmos. While he was there he received a vision from God. This vision is what comprises the book of Revelation.

The apostle is given a message from God, and he is instructed to give it to seven churches. God, in describing Himself to John, declares, "I am Alpha and Omega, the beginning and the ending, saith the Lord, which is, and which was, and which is to come, the Almighty" (Revelation 1:8).

This same expression is reaffirmed in 1:11, when John is instructed to write down the vision he is about to receive. John relates the expression again in 21:6 as the source of his vision.

It is used again in the closing verses of the book: "I am Alpha and Omega, the beginning and the end, the first and the last" (Rev. 22:13).

The Apple of His Eye

We use this expression to give emphasis to something or someone that we hold precious. The person one loves is the apple of his eye.

God saw Israel as the apple of His eye, according to the minor prophet Zechariah: "For thus saith the Lord of Hosts; after the glory hath He sent me into the nations which spoiled you: for He that toucheth you toucheth the apple of His eye" (Zechariah 2:8).

"Apple" in this phrase is a translation into English of the Latin *pupillam,* "the pupil." The pupil was referred to in Old English as the apple because it was thought to be a solid spherical body.

We read in Deut. 32:10 that the Lord kept Israel as the apple of His eye. He guarded Israel with great care. He protected His people. Just as we are careful to keep our eyes from injury, God watches over His people. We must treasure our sight. Without His teachings we are blind; we stumble through life.

Scientists have proven that when we look at a particular person or object for which we have a special feeling, our pupils automatically dilate. That person or object fills the pupils of our eyes. Therefore, this object of our affection becomes the apple of our eye.

In Psalm 17, David beseeches God to "keep me as the apple of the eye, hide me under the shadow of Thy wings." In other words – "Lord, love me and protect me."

We want God to love us, but we aren't always so careful to keep Him as the apple of our eye, as we should.

At Your Wit's End

Do you have times when you feel like you can't think anymore? When you really have to decide something important, but the solution is beyond your ability to comprehend it? You may feel like you're at your wit's end.

The people originally described as being at their "wit's end" were "those that go down to the sea in ships . . ." (Psalm 107:23).

The Psalmist, throughout Psalm 107, repeats the theme, "Oh that men would praise the Lord for His goodness and for His wonderful works to the children of men" (vs. 8, 15, 21 and 31). He draws several comparisons to people in difficult circumstances who cried out to the Lord, and were saved.

He gives a very graphic description of "they that go down to the sea in ships, that do their business in great waters." Beginning in verse 23 and continuing through verse 26, he describes how storms come up and how their ships are mounted on waves and then they go down to the depths. He says, "their soul is melted because of trouble" (v. 26).

Verse 27 then says, "They (those in ships) reel to and fro, and stagger like a drunken man, and are at their wit's end." They don't know what to do. They are beyond their ability to remedy the situation.

Then, says the Psalmist, "They cry unto the Lord in their trouble and He bringeth them out of their distresses" (v. 28).

The next time you think that you are at your wit's end, do what a drowning sailor should do. Call unto the Lord.

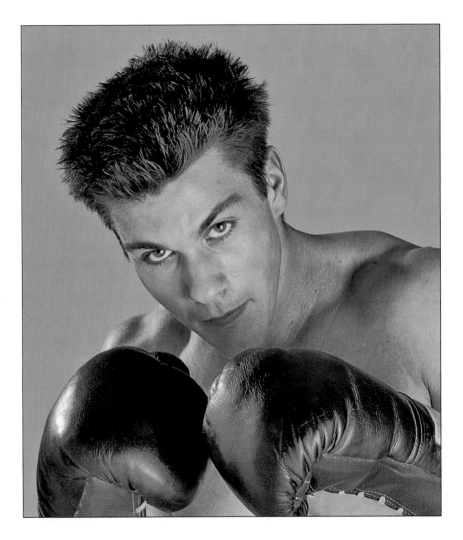

To Beat the Air

Striking out at nothing, as you might in shadow boxing, is "beating the air." Many people who beat the air, though, do it even more intensely than a shadow boxer in practice. They tend to lash out.

Beating the air is like having something you say fall on deaf ears. No one is listening, though the speaker goes on with sound and fury.

Paul uses the expression in an athletic analogy when writing to the Corinthians. He is comparing life to running in a race. He tells the Christians in Corinth that when runners run in a race, only one wins the prize. (1 Corinthians 9:24).

He continues with his comparison, "And every man that striveth for the mastery is temperate in all things. Now they do it to obtain a corruptible crown; but we an incorruptible" (v. 25). In verse 26 he begins to change the analogy from running to fighting for a purpose, "I therefore so run, not as uncertainly; so fight I, not as one that beateth the air . . . "

Paul concludes the chapter, and his analogy, by urging the Corinthians to keep spiritually fit so that they won't lose out and waste their efforts. When we beat the air, we are accomplishing nothing.

Beside Himself

When someone is falling apart emotionally, we call that person unstable. Centuries ago, people believed that when such instability occurred the soul and body had separated. The soul thus separated was then standing beside the body, so a person was said to be standing beside himself.

In the 26th chapter of Acts, Paul, who had been imprisoned in Rome, has an opportunity to recount his Christian conversion in front of King Agrippa and the new governor of Caesarea, Festus. Paul tells Governor Festus and King Agrippa about his encounter with a bright light. He also tells them about having heard a voice speak to him on the road to Damascus. He witnesses to them about Christ and His resurrection from death. Paul tells them he has come to bring light to the Gentiles.

Festus says with a loud voice: "Paul, thou art beside thyself; much learning doth make thee mad" (Acts 26:24).

Festus believes Paul is out of his mind. He suggests that Paul's mind and body are no longer connected.

Concerned friends of Jesus made similar claims. He was so busy attending to the crowds of people who came to Him for miracles, that He wasn't even finding time to eat. "And when His friends heard of it, they went out to lay hold on Him: for they said, He is beside Himself" (Mark 3:21).

While we may not believe that soul and body separate on earth while we are alive, we still say that people are "beside themselves" with grief or worry. We also speak of trying to "keep ourselves together" – but that can only be accomplished with God's help.

Bite the Dust

In cowboy adventures someone is always "biting the dust" – after being shot or thrown from a horse. This saying could also apply to bull riders at the rodeo. It could, therefore, mistakenly be seen as originating in America, but it actually has a much longer history.

It is believed to have been written between 700 B.C. and 1000 B.C.

"To bite the dust" is applied to less than fatal situations today – such as losing an athletic contest, a boyfriend or girlfriend or a business contract. A popular song of our day uses the expression . . . "another one bites the dust" . . . in reference to friendships or relationships that keep falling apart one after the other.

Originally, this expression was a curse.

In Genesis 3:14, the Lord God said to the serpent, "Because thou hast done this, thou art cursed above all cattle, and above every beast of the field; upon thy belly shalt thou go, and dust shalt thou eat all the days of thy life."

The serpent, or snake, used as an instrument of Satan to cause man's rebellion against God, receives God's judgment. He goes from being the subtlest of all beasts that God had made (Genesis 3:1) to the most cursed of all His creation (Genesis 3:14).

Snakes literally bite the dust. They crawl upon the soil constantly and can't help but ingest some of it. The dissected remains of snakes have yielded large deposits of dirt that they swallowed but couldn't spew out.

People who are deceitful are sometimes referred to as snakes in the grass or as slimy as a snake. Spiritually speaking, without repentance – some day, like the snake, they will bite the dust.

The Bitter End

We say that we've come to the bitter end of something when a long, unpleasant series of events is finally concluded. Wordsmiths often trace this expression to the sea.

When the rope or chain that is attached to an anchor of a ship is let out as far as it can go, the post that remains on board (known as the bitt) holds the bitter end of the line. Perhaps this is where we get expressions such as "coming to the end of our rope" or "running out the string."

The bitter end to many people is death, or at least a seemingly endless struggle with a situation or person that eventually comes to some resolve.

In the biblical book of Proverbs, we read about a woman whose lips are sweeter than honey, but whose consequences are just the opposite. "For the lips of a strange woman drop as an honeycomb, and her mouth is smoother than oil: But her end is bitter as wormwood, sharp as a two–edged sword? (Proverbs 5:3, 4).

There are things that appear sweet and good at first, but as the Bible warns, are bitter in the end.

Some people proudly announce that they have "fought it through to the bitter end." The good news of the Scripture is that it's not necessary to have a bitter end if you know Jesus as your Savior and friend.

The Blind Leading the Blind

This saying was first directed toward the Pharisees, the Jewish religious leaders whom Jesus encountered during His earthly ministry. He also called them a "generation of vipers (snakes)."

In Matthew 15:14 we read, "Let them alone, they be blind leaders of the blind. And if the blind lead the blind, both shall fall into the ditch."

This saying has come to be directed at those who give advice to others or who take the lead but who are unfit to do so.

Jesus believed that the Pharisees suffered from spiritual blindness. They could not find their own salvation, but they presumed to lead others toward it. Their blindness was contagious because others were depending on them for spiritual direction.

The comment about their blindness was preceded by a discussion of foods that supposedly defiled a person. Jesus explained that it wasn't what went into a person's mouth that caused them to be defiled, but rather what came out.

The Pharisees thought primarily in physical terms. They had little or no spiritual vision, thus the "blind" label. Nicodemus was a Pharisee who couldn't understand Jesus' teaching on being born again. His mind was stuck on the physical birth (John 3:1–16).

The Pharisees constantly attacked Jesus verbally in public. They questioned His authority and criticized His miracles of healing. They were awed by His insight and spiritual wisdom. They were jealous of His power.

Lest we be blind ourselves, we need to seek after spiritual things. We are admonished in James 1:5, "If any of you lack wisdom, let him ask of God . . . "

Blood Money

There is some revenue that even the government will reject. It is money that some would call guilt money, and others refer to as "blood money." It is tainted in some way. Officials don't want to be connected with it because it reveals their involvement in something that was less than commendable. Certain proceeds from war–captured resources have fallen into this category. It amounts to kicking someone while they are down. It also reveals man's greed at the expense of others.

Judas, one of the disciples of Jesus, went to the chief priests and made them an offer they couldn't refuse. He told them that he was willing to "deliver" Jesus to them. He then asked them what it was worth to them. He settled for 30 pieces of silver (dialogue from Matthew 26:14, 15).

Judas carried out the betrayal by bringing a host of sword–wielding men to the Garden of Gethsemane where Jesus was praying. He betrayed Him with a kiss (Matthew 26:47, 48).

After Jesus was arrested and taken to Pontius Pilate, Judas regretted what he had done. "Then Judas, which had betrayed Him, when he saw that He was condemned, repented himself, and brought again the 30 pieces of silver to the chief priests and the elders, saying, 'I have sinned in that I have betrayed the innocent blood.' And they said, 'What is that to us? See thou to that'" (Matthew 27:3, 4).

Judas, who had received blood money, cast down the 30 pieces of silver and went away and hung himself. "And the chief priests took the silver pieces, and said, 'It is not lawful for to put them into the treasury, because it is the price of blood'" (Matthew 27:6).

By and By

Mothers seem to have an answer for everything. If a child asks his mother when they are going to leave for a place that he is anxious to see, she will often say, "By and by, dear."

Babies who say "bye–bye" are definitely giving a word of farewell.

The expression "by and by" is a little more difficult to pin down. It usually means later, but it is more like "after a while."

An old spiritual hymn has as its chorus, "In the sweet by and by, we shall meet on that beautiful shore . . ." It is speaking of heaven and looking forward to a reunion (at some undefined time) with those we love.

"By and by" is also used in the Parable of the Sower. In Matthew's Gospel, Jesus describes how the devil is always trying to snatch people away from the kingdom of God. He compares people who hear about the kingdom to a seed that falls onto stony ground. The seed begins to grow, but it doesn't take root.

"Yet hath he not root in himself, but dureth for a while: for when tribulation or persecution ariseth because of the Word, by and by he is offended" (Matthew 13:21).

Satan is patient. He will take his opportunities sooner or later. We must be diligent in order to overcome the wiles of the devil.

By the Skin of Your Teeth

Job was despondent. The devil had tested his faith through a series of brutal hardships. God had allowed Satan to tempt Job by whatever means possible, with one exception – he couldn't take his life.

His property was destroyed, his land was taken, his children were killed and he was physically afflicted with an awful illness and with deep depression.

At this point in his life Job declares, "I am escaped with the skin of my teeth" (Job 19:20).

Job has little or nothing left in the world, but there is a glimmer of thankfulness that he has escaped, even by the most narrow of margins. This expression has through the ages continued to be associated with averting disaster. The note of thankfulness also remains.

The saying has had only one modification. The word "by" replaces "with" in modern usage.

Some people say, "I'm going to get into heaven by the skin of my teeth," or "You made the deadline by the skin of your teeth." These expressions remind us of others, such as making something "by a whisker," or "by an eyelash."

Some could argue that the thief on the cross entered into heaven by the skin of his teeth because he made his decision for Christ in his final hours. In truth, we don't get into heaven by any such narrow margin. A person either accepts the salvation God offers or rejects it.

Can a Leopard Change His Spots?

Jeremiah, the prophet, isn't really talking about leopards at all when he asks the question, "Can a leopard change his spots?" (Jeremiah 13:23). The logical response, however, is simply no, he cannot.

The spiritual conclusion, though, is that nothing is impossible with God. Therefore, the leopard's spots can be changed, but he can't do it himself.

Jeremiah also inquires about the possibility of an Ethiopian changing the color of his skin. He is actually drawing an analogy of something that happens to people on the inside rather than the outside.

He is speaking of sin, and he is calling wicked people to repentance. The full verse is, "Can the Ethiopian change his skin, or the leopard his spots? Then may ye also do good that are accustomed to do evil" (Jeremiah 13:23).

In the final verse of the 13th chapter, Jeremiah concludes with two questions that seem more hopeful: "Woe unto thee, O Jerusalem! Wilt thou not be made clean? When shall it once be?" (Jeremiah 13:27).

We often hear that people can change. The conclusion of this questioning expression about a leopard's ability to change his spots seems to be that people can't change their sinful natures, but God can forgive them of their sins when they call on Him and then they will be changed.

Casting Pearls Before Swine

Precious things need to be appreciated. Pigs have no appreciation for pearls. They would simply trash them in mud. They might even turn on you for giving them something that they consider useless.

The expression "casting pearls before swine" is another of Christ's highly visual teaching tools. He wants us to keep this picture in our minds when we deal with things that are holy. He knew that not everyone would accept His message. There were some during His earthly ministry who wouldn't receive the teachings of His disciples. Jesus told the disciples to "shake the dust from your sandals" and move on to another town where people would listen.

In Matthew 7:6, Jesus says, "Give not that which is holy unto the dogs, neither cast ye your pearls before swine, lest they trample them under their feet, and turn again and rend you."

Often the word "pearls" is associated with the word "wisdom." Thus, we say "pearls of wisdom."

While many today would use the advice, "Do not cast pearls before swine," in relation to their material possessions, its original intent was in regard to spiritual things. Sacred things should never be wasted.

Jesus is the "Pearl of great price."

Charity Begins at Home

Child psychologists say that most of a person's attitudes are developed before the age of five. These attitudes and personality traits are learned mostly at home.

The biblical injunction "to train up a child in the way that he should go" is crucial. The family is still the most powerful single influence on society. As family training goes, so goes a nation.

So many things begin in the home that it isn't surprising to hear people say, "Charity begins at home." This enduring expression has unfortunately taken on isolationist overtones. At times it has even been used as the rationale for not giving to people who are in need outside of one's family.

In the original text that Timothy received from Paul as a letter, the word "piety" was used instead of the word "charity."

Paul uses "charity," as a word for love in his first letter to the Corinthians. In the expression, "Charity begins at home," which has become commonly used, the word "charity" means to give or show care. It parallels the word love.

Paul is giving Timothy instruction on Christian caring when he says, "But if any widow have children or nephews, let them learn first to show piety at home, and to requite their parents: for that is good and acceptable before God" (1 Timothy 5:4).

The word "first" in this verse is important, but often overlooked. Caring for others begins in the home, but it doesn't stop there. It reaches out beyond the family to others who are in need.

A Chink in the Armor

When commenting on someone's weakness, we sometimes refer to their shortcoming as a "chink in their armor." This vulnerable personality trait is compared to a crack or an opening, known as a chink, which may occur at the joints in a suit of armor. The chink usually appears when the wearer is under stress during battle. Enemies look for the weaknesses of their opponents, and then try to exploit them.

This phrase, "a chink in the armor," refers to an incident that occurred 900 years before the birth of Christ. It is recorded in the Old Testament book of 1 Kings:

"And a certain man drew a bow at a venture, (by chance) and smote the King of Israel (Ahab) between the joints of the harness: wherefore, (Ahab) said unto the driver of his chariot, Turn thine hand and carry me out of the battle, for I am wounded" (1 Kings 22:34).

Elijah, the prophet, had warned Ahab that he would die in battle as evidence of God's judgment against him. Ahab and his evil wife, Jezebel, had killed Naboth and stolen his property. Elijah said, "Thou has sold thyself to work evil in the sight of the Lord" (1 Kings 21:20).

Ahab denied God's prophecy and went into the battle disguised as a common soldier. For added protection, in addition to his "impenetrable" armor, he had a personal bodyguard. His attempt to make God's prophet a liar was to no avail. The chink in his armor was his own foolish pride.

To Be Cocksure

When someone is so confident that he becomes arrogant, we might refer to him as being "cocksure." This saying is akin to "dead right," "dead certain" and "without a doubt."

It sounds like a hunting term that could refer to the game being sought, or even to the weapon being used. Logically, we should be cocksure if we ever plan to use a rifle. We don't want to have an itchy "trigger–finger" or cock the gun too soon.

In the Bible, it was Peter, the disciple, who acted like he was cocksure. He was often impulsive and quick to act. He didn't seem to learn from his experience of falling in the water in the Sea of Galilee, after briefly walking on it toward Jesus. His confidence at first was rightly placed in Christ, but when he relied on his own resources, he failed.

At the Last Supper, Jesus explained what was going to happen to Him soon. Peter interrupted Him with a question . . . "Lord, whither goest Thou? Jesus answered him, 'Whither I go, thou canst not follow Me now; but thou shalt follow Me afterwards.' Peter said unto Him, 'Lord why cannot I follow Thee now? I will lay down my life for Thy sake.' Jesus answered him, 'Wilt thou lay down thy life for My sake? Verily, verily I say unto thee, The cock shall not crow till thou hast denied Me thrice'" (John 13:36–38).

Jesus was warning Peter not to be so cocksure of his own strength in dealings with the things that were about to happen.

John 18:27 records what did happen shortly after Christ's arrest, when Peter was being asked questions about knowing Jesus: "Peter then denied again: (a third time) and immediately the cock crowed."

Cry Me a River

To lament is to be sorrowful and often involves crying. The book of the Lamentations of Jeremiah is very short (five chapters), but a lot of crying occurs within its pages. This book earned Jeremiah the name "The Weeping Prophet."

The colorful expression, "Cry me a river," comes from Lamentations. It has made its way into countless ballads, love songs and poems through the years. One mournful lover sang sorrowfully, "Cry me a river, I cried a river over you . . ."

Lamentations 2:11 opens with this phrase, "Mine eyes do fail with tears . . ." Jeremiah is sorrowing over Jerusalem's misery for her sins because God has pronounced His judgment upon the inhabitants of the city.

Jeremiah goes on to say, "Their heart cried unto the Lord, O wall of the daughter of Zion, let tears run down like a river day and night: give thyself no rest . . ." (Lamentations 2:18).

Tears are still seen today at a wall in the city of Jerusalem. These are not the tears of melancholy love songs, but the deep tears of repentance and awe–filled worship. Those who go to the "Wailing Wall" together are reverently crying a river unto God, who sees our tears and knows the desires of our hearts.

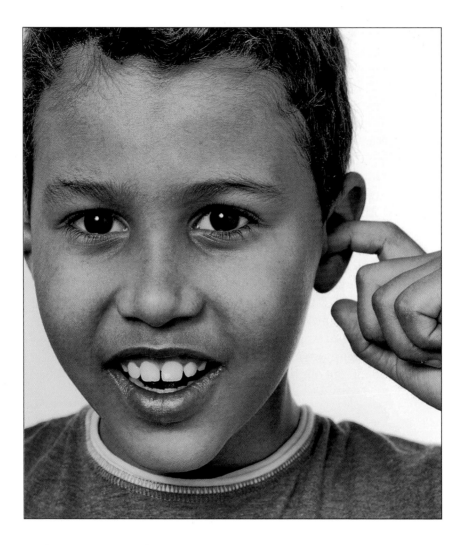

Deaf as an Adder

Most people use the expression, "deaf as a doornail," which traces back to the scriptural original "deaf as an adder." An adder is a snake that apparently only hears what it chooses to hear. According to the Bible's description, an adder couldn't be charmed unless it wanted to be.

When we use this expression nowadays we aren't referring to people who are hearing impaired. We are directing our frustration at a child or a mate who seems to have selective hearing. They hear the call to supper, but are seemingly deaf when asked to take out the garbage.

In Psalm 58:3–5, the wicked are compared to snakes that will not be charmed. They hear only what they choose to, and they like having their own way. They do whatever they choose to, following the whims of their self–will.

The Bible says of the wicked, "Their poison is like the poison of a serpent: They are like the deaf adder that stoppeth her ear" (Psalm 58:4).

When people are acting selfishly, they don't want to hear what other people have to say. Spiritual selfishness will make us as deaf as a doornail to the things of God.

A Den of Thieves

A father advised his son, "You don't want to go in there, that place is a den of thieves." The phrase was so colorful and curious to the boy that he later went into the tavern to see it for himself. He discovered it was a hangout for local gamblers and bookmakers.

The boy's fascination with Ali Baba and the 40 thieves had captured his imagination, but the phrase doesn't usually apply so literally. It is a warning about the character of particular establishments or homes, and sometimes it applies to shady businesses.

Originally, Jesus used the expression in referring to the Temple, the holy place of worship. He used it just after He turned the tables on the moneychangers.

"And He [Jesus] taught, saying unto them, 'Is it not written, My house shall be called of all nations the house of prayer? but ye (money changers and animal sellers) have made it a den of thieves'" (Mark 11:17).

The actions and remarks of Jesus didn't sit well with the scribes and Pharisees. The Bible says that they feared Him, and they went looking for a way to destroy Him. Shortly afterward He was crucified on a cross between two thieves.

Doubting Thomas

S ome people need to have all their ducks in a row – like the supervisor who assigned one of his employees to set up 12 tables in a dining area. When the job was complete, the supervisor asked if the correct number of tables had been arranged. The employee said "yes." Then the supervisor went to the dining area and counted the tables.

While the supervisor's doubts were motivated by a lack of trust, the expression "doubting Thomas," came from a lack of faith.

Most people know that the phrase relates to a disciple of Jesus. Thomas was not with the disciples when Jesus first appeared to them following His Resurrection from the dead.The disciples later assured Thomas that Christ had appeared to them, and that He was alive.

The statement that made Thomas infamous is contained in John 20:25, "The other disciples therefore said unto him [Thomas], We have seen the Lord. But he said unto them, Except I shall see in His hands the print of the nails, and put my finger into the print of the nails, and thrust my hand into His side, I will not believe."

Eight days later, Jesus appeared again to the disciples. This time Thomas was with them. "Jesus saith unto him, Thomas, because thou hast seen Me, thou hast believed: blessed (happy) are they that have not seen, and yet have believed" (John 20:29).

A Drop in the Bucket

When something is so small that it is insignificant, it is said to be "a drop in the bucket." It may be an item, an event or someone's contribution to a project.

The reference to something as "only a drop in the bucket" doesn't make it worthless. The implication is that the contribution helps, but in comparison to the whole, it matters little. We are often told in our society that "every little bit helps."

Isaiah, the prophet, used this expression to compare the nations of the world with the magnificence and majesty of God when he said, "Behold, the nations are as a drop of a bucket, and are counted as the small dust of the balance: behold, He taketh up the isles as a very little thing" (Isaiah 40:15).

Isaiah's message wasn't meant to be a put–down, but rather a message of consolation and encouragement. He wanted to show God as great and glorious.

The message was aimed at those who were being held captive in Babylon. Isaiah was telling them to keep on trusting God for their deliverance. He wanted them to see that even though their enemies were strong – God was all–powerful.

If we ever get discouraged with the world's situation we should remember this word of encouragement. No matter how powerful the nations of the world may become, they are only a drop in the bucket when compared with God and His omnipotent power.

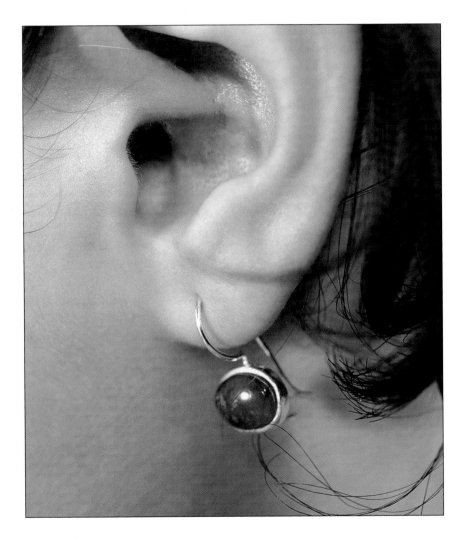

Earmarked

When we say something is earmarked we mean it has been set apart for a special purpose. In the Bible, we read of men being earmarked voluntarily as bondservants nearly 1,500 years before the birth of Jesus Christ. ". . . his master shall bore his ear through with an aul and he shall serve him forever" (Exodus 21:6).

This verse refers to a Hebrew law that allowed a servant who had completed a six–year period of servanthood to be set free in the seventh year. If the servant, however, chose voluntarily to stay and serve his master, he was allowed to do so with full benefits.

His Hebrew sponsor usually afforded him great kindness. The servant was marked with a hole through his ear lobe, which distinguished him from other people who served without choice.

The Israelites, who had been servants themselves, knew the value of showing kindness toward them. The loyalty of the earmarked bondservant was the reward a master received for showing love.

David refers to this bondservant relationship in Psalm 40:6 when he says, ". . . mine ears hast Thou opened . . . " He isn't speaking of having open ears to hear well, but an opening in his earlobes to signify bondservant status.

In Psalm 84:10, he says, "I had rather be a doorkeeper in the house of my God, than to dwell in the tents of wickedness."

At the Eleventh Hour

S omeone who is spared death by execution at the last possible moment receives an "eleventh hour" reprieve. Decisions left to the last moment are called eleventh hour decisions because of a parable that Jesus told in the 20th chapter of the Gospel of Matthew.

This "earthly story with a heavenly meaning" told of a householder who went out early in the morning to hire laborers to work in his vineyard. He agreed to pay the laborers an acceptable wage.

"And about the eleventh hour he went out, and found others standing idle, and saith unto them, Why stand ye here all day idle?" (Matthew 20:6). They told him it was because no man had hired them.

The head of the vineyard told them to go to work in the fields, and whatever was right to pay them, he would.

When the day was over he paid all the workers the same amount that the earliest workers had agreed to in the morning, even the eleventh hour crew (Matthew 20:9). Many of the workers grumbled, thinking they deserved more because they'd worked a longer day. The man who hired them said he'd paid them what they had agreed to, and they shouldn't be upset because everyone was treated the same.

On the Day of Judgment, the number of years that you've trusted in Jesus will not determine whether you get into heaven. It will be decided on whether you know Him as Savior on that day.

The Ends of the Earth

C olumbus told the people of his time that the earth was round. Many people feared that he was wrong. They believed that the world was flat and that there was an ending point, an edge, at which they would fall off if they ventured near it. Some very learned men of his time held to the "flat–world" theory. Indeed, there is still a Flat World Society that believes the pictures taken from space are all part of a hoax.

Some expressions from the Bible could have added to the confusion of the flat–world believers. For example, Isaiah 11:12 reads, "And He shall set up an ensign for the nations, and shall assemble the outcasts of Israel, and gather together the dispersed of Judah from the four corners of the earth."

Things that are round don't have corners. So, if the earth were round, why would Isaiah talk about God gathering the "dispersed of Judah" from "the four corners of the earth"? Newscasters and ordinary folks, like you and me, still use this colorful expression. But we know the earth is round, don't we?

In Psalm 98:3, referring to God, the Psalmist says, "He hath remembered His mercy and His truth toward the house of Israel: all the ends of the earth have seen the salvation of our God."

The "ends of the earth"? Things that are round don't have endings. Some people think this "ends of the earth" expression originated with romantic love songs, and it was considered by many to be the length that lovers would go for each other. It's actually the length that God has gone for each of us.

An Eye for an Eye

Retaliation is what keeps wars going. Even parents who are told by their child that another child "hit me" are prone to say, "Go hit him back." Retaliation is a knee–jerk reaction that generally feels like justice.

Allegiances to this natural human response and an Old Testament admonition of an "eye for an eye" have often kept the battle for capital punishment on our ballots. People want to feel like they have somehow gotten even for a wrong that has been done to them or to someone they love.

Governments establish the laws and carry out capital punishment. People are not free to take vengeance into their own hands. After due process of the law, punishment is meted out that, hopefully, fits the crime.

The original source of the "eye for an eye" quote is Exodus 21:22–25: "If men strive and hurt a woman with child, so that her fruit depart from her, and yet no mischief follow: he shall be surely punished, according as the woman's husband will lay upon him; and he shall pay as the judges determine. And if any mischief follow, then thou shalt give life for life, eye for eye, tooth for tooth, hand for hand, foot for foot, burning for burning, wound for wound, stripe for stripe."

Jesus, in His Sermon on the Mount, referred to this practice when he said, "Ye have heard that it hath been said, An eye for an eye, and a tooth for a tooth: But I say unto you, That ye resist not evil: but whosoever shall smite thee on thy right check, turn to him the other also" (Matthew 5:38, 39).

The law of non–retaliation can only be learned spiritually. Our human tendency to want to get even can never be satisfied in any other way. Paul the Apostle reminds us, "Vengeance is mine, I will repay, saith the Lord" (Romans 12:19).

Far Be It from Me

T his dramatic disclaimer, "far be it from me," has remained as a commonly used phrase for centuries. It is still used in its original form, word for word.

When we use "far be it from me," we mean "it's not for me to do," or "I wouldn't think of doing it."

In the second book of Samuel, it is used by one of King David's key military men, Joab. He was sent out by the king to pursue and destroy a man named Sheba, who was the leader of a rebellion against the king.

Joab and his fellow–warriors left Jerusalem and went throughout all the tribes of Israel in pursuit of Sheba and his rebels. When they came to a city called Abel of Beth Maacah, Joab's men began to batter the walls of the city.

A voice of a woman cried out from the city, calling for Joab to come forward so she could speak with him. The woman, whom the Bible doesn't name, is described as a very wise woman. She says to Joab, "I am one of them that are peaceable and faithful in Israel: thou seekest to destroy a city and a mother in Israel: why wilt thou swallow up the inheritance of the Lord?"

And Joab answered and said, "Far be it from me, that I should swallow up or destroy" (2 Samuel 20:19–20).

He says the Israelites don't want to destroy the city, but they want Sheba, who is hiding within their walls. The woman goes back into the city and gives this information to the city's leaders. Soon after this discussion, they throw the head of Sheba from the city wall. The city is spared and Joab takes Sheba's head to King David.

Feet of Clay

If someone is strong in most areas of their life, but proves to be weak or vulnerable in a previously undetected area, we might say they have "feet of clay." This physical reference is actually directed toward a weak spiritual foundation.

We read in the Old Testament about King Nebuchadnezzar of Assyria who had a disturbing dream. It bothered him so much that he couldn't remember the details when he woke up. He called for his wise men and demanded that they recount the dream for him and explain its meaning or they would be put to death.

The prophet Daniel did what King Nebuchadnezzar's wise men couldn't. He had a vision and he was able to interpret the king's dream, which called for the destruction of Assyria as recorded in Daniel 2.

There was a statue in the dream with a golden head, silver chest and arms, brass thighs and belly, legs of iron and feet made partly of iron and partly of clay. The statue fell apart. It blew away in the wind when a stone struck the feet, its weakest part.

Weakness, even when hidden, can lead to destruction for a person, a family, or even a nation.

This phrase can apply to anyone, but it is particularly used to denounce failed leadership. When a leader of a group or of a nation fails to live up to the need for strength, there is great disappointment.

A Fly in the Ointment

Just when you think everything is perfect, something goes wrong. At first it may seem like a small problem, but it ruins the whole effort.

Insects in ointments (creams, perfumes) just won't work. In the same way that a small ink stain on a long, flowing gown makes the dress unwearable, so one dissenting vote on a jury makes the jury unworkable.

We may, at times, be tempted to ignore the small things. Things that may appear small when standing alone can, however, become very noticeable when inappropriately placed.

Solomon is issuing a warning to guard against acting foolishly when he writes, "Dead flies cause the ointment of the apothecary to send forth a stinking savour: so doth little folly him that is in reputation for wisdom and honor" (Ecclesiastes 10:1).

Someone's folly may be his or her temper. People can undo a lot of good things when they lose their temper, no matter how long they may have been acting in a calm and reasonable manner. The "blow–up" becomes the "fly in the ointment." People remember it long afterward despite a lengthy record of disciplined behavior.

The "fly" may be a flaw in a person's character or personality. A person who has spent his whole life in one career may be forced to leave it because racial prejudice or some hidden vice was suddenly revealed. The revelation of such attitudes or activities brings people down.

Giving Up the Ghost

Passing from this life into the next is referred to in many ways. Because people have trouble talking about death, euphemisms are often used to describe the occurrence.

The spiritual euphemism for death, "to give up the ghost," is sometimes also used to signify the end of things like projects or companies. It comes from a question asked by Job.

In Job 14:10, we read, "But man dieth, and wasteth away: yea, man giveth up the ghost, and where is he?"

This is part of Job's response to Zophar, one of three friends who have come to visit him in his affliction. Job said to Zophar that he longed to speak to God to obtain reasons for his troubles, but that he wished his friends would keep their advice to themselves.

In sharing his philosophy with his friends, Job asks the penetrating question, "If a man dies, shall he live again?" (Job 14:14). It is in this context that he refers to the spirit (the old English word is ghost) separating from the body, or giving up the ghost.

Job's hope is that the spirit of man, like the Holy Spirit (also called the Holy Ghost) is eternal and will return to God from whence it came.

Giving the Shirt off Your Back

Generosity is a highly regarded trait. People who have a gift for giving are always appreciated. While some people have a standard donation or gift level for every project throughout the year, others give beyond what is expected.

When someone "gives the shirt off his back," it means that he gives to the point where he isn't thinking about himself. His concern for others is so great that he ignores his own comfort. He gives sacrificially, but he does it in love.

Jesus, God the Father's gift to us, taught that love is shown by actions. In Matthew 5:40, Jesus tells His followers that there may come a time when someone demands their coat and even sues them for it. He tells them to respond to such demands by being willing to give their shirt as well, even though it hasn't been requested.

The expression "keep your shirt on" is unrelated to this saying. It means to hold one's temper. It was once considered customary to take off one's shirt when getting into a fist–fight. So, literally, keep your shirt on, but figuratively and spiritually – "give the shirt off your back" for others.

Going the Extra Mile

"It's not worth my job to do it," a man in England said. An American, seeking an interpretation of this statement, discovered that it was similar to an expression used in the United States: "It's not in my job description."

One sage has advised, "If you only do that which you must, you soon will show signs of rust."

People often complain that it is hard to find good service in our modern times. Self–service seems to be the rule in most places, but many service–related workers seem to do only what they are required to do and no more.

A lot of people are surprised to learn that it was Jesus who added the expression, "going the extra mile" to our language. During His Sermon on the Mount, He said, "And whosoever shall compel thee to go a mile, go with him twain" (Matthew 5:41).

When someone is willing to do more than they are asked to do, they are cherished. We have high regard for "self–starters." Going beyond what is expected takes motivation. Christ taught that you don't count the cost when you do something motivated by love.

Jesus follows up His second mile advice with a command that disputes Shakespeare's counsel of "Neither a borrower, nor a lender be." Christ says, "Give to him that asketh thee, and from him that would borrow of thee, turn not thou away" (Matthew 5:42).

Going to the Dogs

When someone or something is in a state of decline we might say they are "going to the dogs." Even though dogs are cherished as pets, they aren't treated kindly in most expressions. We hear people say, "you dirty dog," or that someone is "living like a dog."

Jesus, who advised His disciples not to give holy things to dogs (Gentiles), was confronted with a situation where He tried to put this teaching into practice.

A Canaanite woman approached Jesus while He was traveling with His disciples along the coast of Tyre and Sidon. She cried out to Him, but He didn't answer her. Later His disciples came to talk with Him because the woman was following them and she wouldn't take "no" for an answer.

Jesus explained to the disciples that He had come for the "lost sheep of the house of Israel." The woman, who was a Gentile, persisted. She came to Him and worshipped Him and said, "Lord, help me" (Matthew 15:25).

But He answered and said, "It is not meet to take the children's bread and to cast it to the dogs" (Matthew 15:26).

Her request to Christ was not for herself, but for her daughter who was ill. Jesus told her that she had great faith and that she had answered well when she said, "Truth, Lord: yet the dogs eat of the crumbs which fall from their masters' table" (Matthew 15:27). Her daughter was made well through the power of Christ, as a result of a mother's faith.

Good Riddance

As children we sometimes became angry with our friends who had decided not to play with us. We would then taunt each other, usually in two opposing groups.

One of the things we seemed to delight in yelling back and forth to each other was the expression, "Good riddance to bad rubbish."

Adults use the term "good riddance" to express their happiness at finally being finished with something or someone. It ranges from a broken lawn mower, replaced by a new one, to a difficult neighbor who ultimately decided to move elsewhere.

In the prophet Zephaniah's time, God was becoming increasingly impatient with people who thought of Jehovah as wishy–washy. The minor prophet records, "And it shall come to pass at that time, that I will search Jerusalem with candles, and punish the men that are settled on their lees (warm beds): that say in their heart, The Lord will not do good, neither will He do evil" (Zephaniah 1:12).

God was going to strike out against idolatry. He had told the people they should have no other gods, but they grew lax and God took action.

"Neither their silver nor their gold shall be able to deliver them in the day of the Lord's wrath; but the whole land shall be devoured by the fire of His (God's) jealousy: for He shall make even a speedy riddance of all them that dwell in the land" (Zephaniah 1:18).

It wasn't only a case of "good riddance" – it was God's riddance of those who wouldn't obey His commands.

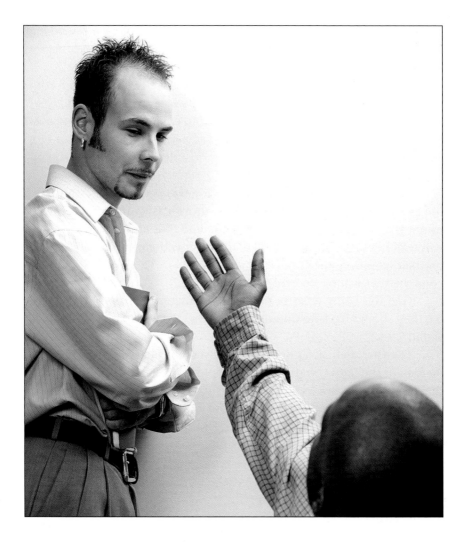

Good Samaritan

Someone whose car breaks down on a rural roadway is grateful for any help received from a passerby. In relating a story of assistance from a complete stranger, people often refer to that person as a Good Samaritan.

Few people stop to think about the origin of the word Samaritan. They may have always used it because they heard their parents or their grandparents use it before them. It's just always been the right word for the circumstance.

The Samaritans were once a hated people. They were a group of Jewish people in northern Israel who had been conquered by Assyria. Their men were killed and their women raped during the attack. When they became mixed culturally and religiously, they could no longer worship at the temple in Jerusalem. They built their own temple in Samaria and held somewhat different beliefs from other Jews. Animosity prevailed on both sides.

Jesus made a Samaritan man the hero of one of his parables, to the consternation of the religious leaders of that time. In the story, recorded in Luke 10:30–35, Jesus tells of a man who was traveling on the road from Jerusalem to Jericho when he was jumped by thieves and robbers. They stole everything he had, leaving him "half dead."

Two people came along, a priest and a Levite, both religious men. They passed the man by. Then a Samaritan came. He had "compassion on him." He bound up the man's wounds, put him on his own animal and took him to an inn. The Samaritan paid for the man to stay at the inn. He also told the innkeeper that if he needed more money, he would settle up with him when he came back that way in the near future. Ever since, complete strangers who help others are called Good Samaritans.

The Grim Reaper

People don't like to use the word death. They talk about loved ones "passing away," or "being gone." The church has terms of its own, such as "having been called Home," "gone to Glory," or "entering a better life."

The Bible speaks of heaven and hell, but few people want to discuss the latter. Consistently, polls show that far more people believe in heaven than in hell.

The term, "grim reaper," while somewhat antiquated, is still understood to mean death and judgment. It has sometimes served as a substitute phrase for people who want to avoid words like death or judgment.

Jesus told a parable about the planting of good seed that would grow into productive wheat. He said that an enemy came late at night and planted useless weeds among the wheat seeds. The servants of the landowner came and told him about the weeds growing up among the wheat. They asked if they should try to uproot the weeds, but he told them to leave them alone to grow together.

Christ concludes the parable with this, "Let both grow together until the harvest: and in the time of harvest I will say to the reapers, Gather ye together first the tares (weeds), and bind them in bundles to burn them: but gather the wheat into my barn" (Matt. 13:30).

When the disciples asked Jesus for an explanation of this parable, he told them, "The enemy that sowed them (the tares) is the devil; the harvest is the end of the world; and the reapers are the angels" (Matthew 13:39).

This story of final judgment paints a cheerful ending for the good seed, but a grim reaping for that which is worthless.

The Handwriting on the Wall

When we say, "the handwriting is on the wall," we are speaking of a sign or a series of signs that point to difficulties ahead. Nowadays people use this phrase when talking about such things as the possible loss of a job. Originally, the statement was a forecast of doom.

The phrase refers to an event that is recorded in the fifth chapter of the book of Daniel. It is directed toward Belshazzar, who succeeded his father, Nebuchadnezzar, as king of the Chaldeans.

Belshazzar ordered his servants to put together a great feast to celebrate his ascension to the throne. He wanted the feast to be a demonstration of his great power.

In an effort to show his guests that he was in complete command of the Jews, he brought out the golden vessels that had been taken from the temple in Jerusalem. He desecrated these vessels by drinking his wine from them and by allowing others to do the same.

As soon as the people drank from these cups, there "came forth fingers of a man's hand and wrote over against the candlestick upon the plaister of the wall of the king's palace . . ." The words were these: "MENE, MENE, TEKEL, UPHARSIN" (Daniel 5:5, 25).

The king, seeing this, was astounded and frightened. He sought an interpretation of the words. The only person who could provide one was the Hebrew prophet, Daniel.

Daniel told him that MENE meant God had numbered his kingdom and finished it. TEKEL, he was told, meant that he had been weighed in the balances and found wanting. UPHARSIN indicated that the kingdom was divided and would be given over to the Medes and Persians.

That night Belshazzar was killed. His kingdom was taken over by Darius the Mede. In his pride, the king had advertised his drunken feast too well. His enemies were waiting outside the city to seize him.

Head and Shoulders Above the Rest

People who have personal qualities that make them stand out among their peers are sometimes described as being "head and shoulders above the rest." This phrase isn't used in the physical sense nowadays, except by basketball coaches. It relates to character, leadership and ability. It can be applied to any area of a person's life where they excel.

Saul, the first King of Israel, was described as being head and shoulders above the rest. Despite the description, God didn't want Saul, or anyone else, to lead His people. The children of Israel had insisted on having a king, even though God wanted them to depend solely on Him for guidance.

Eventually, the high priest Samuel was directed by God to seek out Saul so that Samuel could anoint him as king. Samuel went to the home of a man named Kish. This man had several sons, one of whom was Saul.

Here is how the Bible describes him: "And he (Kish) had a son, whose name was Saul, a choice young man, and goodly: and there was not among the children of Israel a goodlier person than he: from his shoulders and upward he was higher than any of the people" (1 Samuel 9:2).

This verse combines Saul's personal quality of goodness with a physical description of him as being higher (taller) than any of the people, from the shoulders up.

Nowadays the expression refers principally to someone's inner abilities by saying that they are "head and shoulders above the rest."

To Be Heartsick

People who are disappointed in romance are sometimes said to be "heartsick." Parents also know periods of heartsickness during times of concern for their children. They, and others in difficult or disappointing circumstances, are also referred to as being "downhearted."

The terms "heartsick" and "downhearted" aren't related to the physical organ in the center of our chests, but refer to the state of our emotions.

Even though the expression isn't used to describe cardiovascular problems, continued heartsickness can lead to depression and physical problems. Our emotions can seriously affect our physical condition.

When we feel heartsick, we also sometimes feel hopeless. The Bible says that when we have put aside hopeful feelings, we will become heartsick. "Hope deferred maketh the heart sick: but when the desire cometh, it is a tree of life" (Proverbs 13:12).

The first reference to the heart in the Bible is in Genesis 6:5 when God declares, "every imagination of the thoughts of his (man's) heart was only evil continually."

Solomon, who introduces us to heartsickness in the Proverbs, also offers us a solution.

"A merry heart doeth good like a medicine . . ." (Proverbs 17:22).

To Hide Your Light Under a Bushel

Many people are talented, but they are afraid to show others their talents or their personalities. If someone has ability that isn't being used, that person is said to be "hiding it under a bushel." This reference comes from a statement Jesus made to His disciples as part of the Sermon on the Mount.

Jesus said, "Ye are the light of the world. A city that is set on a hill cannot be hid. Neither do men light a candle, and put it under a bushel, but on a candlestick; and it giveth light onto all that are in the house" (Matthew 5:14–15).

Christ encouraged His disciples to let their light shine before others, so that the people who saw them and their actions would give the glory to God.

Candlelight (fire) is transferable. Theoretically, one candle can be used to light all other candles in the world. A candle that is covered is denied oxygen – it suffocates and its light is put out.

While it is very difficult for some people to speak openly, it is the only way that their light can be shared clearly. Hopefully the importance of the Light of the World, Jesus Christ, will motivate us to forget our personal fears so that we can keep our spiritual light shining for Him.

To Be High Handed

After scoring a touchdown, players in the National Football League go through a series of modern rituals. Some dance, others spike the ball and some even do back flips. Another of these emotional demonstrations is called the "high five." It occurs when the players jump into the air and slap the palms of their right hands together.

This innovation is actually a variation on an old theme. Raising the arms and hands high into the air seems to be almost a universal sign of victory and triumph.

In the book of Numbers, the Jews were considered "high handed" by their enemies, the Egyptians, as they escaped triumphantly under God's protection. "And they departed from Rameses in the first month, . . . on the morrow after the passover the children of Israel went out with an high hand in the sight of all the Egyptians" (Numbers 33:3). Perhaps the Egyptians perceived this demonstration as arrogant and overbearing.

Originally, the high hand was an acknowledgement aimed heavenward. It was a sign of God's power.

Today when we use the term "high handed," it is with a sense of scorn. Someone who is high handed is seen as flaunting his or her power. It is associated with taunting, teasing and conceit. It is like pouring salt into a wound.

Today's victors usually intend that their high fives will serve as a sign of their own superiority. Human beings have claimed the high hand, which was originally directed toward God, and their opponents hate them for it.

In the Christian community the raising of our hands skyward should be a recognition of God and his greatness. As one Christian chorus encourages us to do, "Let us lift up holy hands unto the Lord."

Hope Against Hope

Hopeless is an overused word. It is too often used to describe a person or a situation that may be far better off than we think. We are often too quick to employ a word with very strong implications.

Hope is a futuristic word. It applies only to what is ahead. We can't hope in the past because it is already gone. We usually find hope in our children, and our children's children. Our greatest source of hope is God.

Paul, in his letter to the Romans. uses an interesting phrase to describe Abraham. His subject is justification by faith, and he uses the Old Testament patriarch as his model of someone who lived by faith in God. (Abraham and his wife Sarah are also prominent among the names listed in the faith chapter, the 11th chapter of Hebrews).

Abraham's situation looked hopeless. He was old, his wife was well past her childbearing years, and they wanted a son to carry on their family line.

Paul says of Abraham, "who against hope believed in hope, that he might become the father of many nations" (Romans 4:18).

When it appeared that all hope was gone, Abraham put his hope in hope. We still use the expression "hope against hope" today when a situation appears to have very little chance of being resolved.

Abraham moved from hope to faith in God. God kept his promise and a son was born to Abraham and Sarah, named Isaac. He became the descendant who would lead the children of Israel to become a great nation.

A House Divided Will Not Stand

During the U.S. Civil War, President Abraham Lincoln was deeply concerned that the country remain united. He knew there were family members from the North who were fighting against family members from the South. Sometimes brothers were on opposite sides in the same battle.

President Lincoln told the people of the United States and the people of the Confederate States that "a nation divided against itself will not stand." His inspiration for this statement may well have come during his daily Bible reading.

The scribes and Pharisees that Jesus contended with during his earthly ministry were always looking for a way to destroy Him. Mark's Gospel records an incident where these religious teachers, whom Jesus called hypocrites, started to spread rumors among the people about Him. They said that he had Beelzebub (the prince of devils) within Him. They reasoned that it was by the power of the devil that He could bring about healing and cast out devils.

Jesus confronted them on their charges. "And he (Jesus) called them unto Him and said unto them in parables, How can Satan cast out Satan? And if a kingdom be divided against itself, that kingdom cannot stand. And if a house be divided against itself, that house cannot stand" (Mark 3:23, 25).

Forgiveness and reconciliation are essential if people are to be united. Thinking that we can live at peace in a divided house would only be deceiving ourselves.

In Over Our Heads

When our abilities don't match our challenges we sometimes admit that we are "in over our heads." We can get into awkward situations or overwhelming circumstances very quickly.

A woman at the ocean nearly drowned when she stepped from a small sandbar. One moment she was enjoying all the pleasures of being at the beach, the next she was in over her head, fighting for survival. The undertow prevented her from regaining her footing, but fortunately another swimmer saw her arms waving and rescued her.

Some people discover to their horror that they are in over their heads financially, and waves of debt come crashing over them. It's easy to get swamped if we're not careful with credit cards or loans. Sometimes our despair is caused by the loss of a job or an accident.

The expression "in over our heads" comes from the prophet Ezra, who is speaking to God about sin when he says, "O my God: I am ashamed and blush to lift up my face to Thee, my God, for our iniquities are increased over our head and our trespass is grown up into the heavens" (Ezra 9:6).

A similar admission of being overwhelmed by personal sin is echoed by King David in Psalm 38:4 when he says, "For mine iniquities are gone over mine head: as an heavy burden they are too heavy for me."

Jesus says, "Come unto me, all ye that labour and are heavy laden and I will give you rest" (Matthew 11:28).

If you're in over your head, reach out to Jesus; you'll find perfect rest in Him.

In the Twinkling of an Eye

How can you measure the twinkling of an eye? It happens instantaneously. Quicker than the time it takes to snap your fingers. Car accidents are sometimes said to happen this quickly. The driver might say it happened in the blinking of an eye, sometimes the blinking of an eyelash. Some cars have been described as "coming out of nowhere."

Paul, in writing to the Corinthian Church, admits that he is dealing with great mysteries when he speaks of the things of God.

The apostle is trying to decipher between things physical and things spiritual. "Now this I say, brethren, that flesh and blood cannot inherit the kingdom of God; neither doth corruption inherit incorruption" (1 Corinthians 15:50).

Paul seems to be saying – here is the physical part, we can all understand that. Then he seems to suggest that they hold onto their hats because he's going to delve into the spiritual and eternal part, which is not so easily defined.

"Behold I show you a mystery; We shall not all sleep, but we shall all be changed. In a moment, in the twinkling of an eye, at the last trump: for the trumpet shall sound, and the dead shall be raised incorruptible, and we shall be changed" (1 Corinthians 15: 51, 52).

According to Paul, we should all be ready when Christ returns because things are going to happen quickly. More quickly than the "twinkling of an eye."

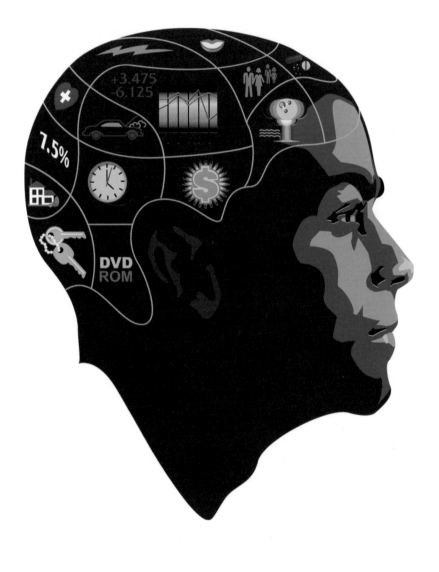

+3.475
-6.125

7.5%

DVD
ROM

In Your Right Mind

S omeone has jokingly said that because left–handed people think in the right sphere of their brain and right–handed people think in their left sphere, left–handed people are the only ones who are in their "right mind" most of the time.

When we say that someone is in their "right mind" we mean that they are sane. If you are not in your right mind, you are thought to be mentally ill.

The word "right" seems to have always been correct, while "left" seems wrong to some folks. The word "sinister" is from Latin and it refers to the left hand. The expressions "all right" and "left out" show something of the preferential treatment that "right" gets.

Even the Bible shows a deep regard for the word right, as in right-eousness. Who's ever heard of "lefteousness?"

We also need to remember that another opposite of right is wrong, so that someone who isn't in their right mind is in their wrong mind. Jesus encountered a man who was possessed by demons. The people thought that he wasn't in his right mind.

The man's name was Legion because so many evil spirits inhabited his body. He lived among the tombs. Each night he would go outside crying, screaming and cutting himself with sharp rocks.

Jesus commanded the demons to leave this man's body and enter into a great herd of 2,000 pigs. The pigs ran down a steep hill into water and they perished (Mark 5:13).

Although the man returned home "in his right mind" and praised God for healing him, witnesses to this extraordinary event were con-sumed by fear and pleaded with Jesus to leave the area.

Itching Ears

According to some people, an itching palm is supposed to mean one of two things: you are about to meet someone if your right hand itches, or you'll soon receive a gift of money if your left hand does.

Superstitions count for very little, and should be ignored.

Prophecy, on the other hand, is valuable.

Paul the Apostle told Timothy that a time would come when people would have "itching ears."

The instructions Timothy received from Paul were to "Preach the Word; be instant in season, out of season; reprove, rebuke, exhort with all longsuffering and doctrine" (2 Timothy 4:2).

Paul then gave him a warning. "For the time will come when they will not endure sound doctrine; but after their own lusts shall they heap to themselves teachers, having itching ears" (2 Timothy 4:3).

You've probably heard someone say that they were "itching" to hear what someone else had to tell them. Paul's warning is that someday people will just want to be entertained. They will only hear what is pleasing to them.

He goes on to say that they will turn their ears from the truth and will turn to fables instead. In our time there are a host of false messengers with mixed messages. It's important for us to be discerning about the things we read or see rendered as truth.

The Kiss of Death

If the coach visits a professional athlete in his room during training camp, it is seen as a bad sign. It usually means that the player will not be making the team that season. Coaches are supposed to be close to their players, but a visit away from the playing field usually means bad news. Fellow players have even been known to call it "the kiss of death."

Workers in other professions are also wary of untimely visits from supervisors or people from personnel. They know that some confidential meetings, even over lunch, can spell danger.

Jesus was praying in the Garden of Gethsemane when Judas, His disciple, appeared with a great multitude of people who were carrying swords and sticks. "Now he that betrayed Him gave them a sign, saying, Whomsoever I shall kiss, that same is He; hold Him fast. And forthwith he came to Jesus, and said, Hail, Master; and kissed Him" (Matthew 26:48, 49).

It wasn't unusual for men in the Middle East to greet one another with a kiss on the cheek. It is still common there today. Jesus responds to Judas and his greeting by calling him "friend" and by asking him why he'd come (even though Jesus knew he had come to betray Him). At that moment the men with the swords seized Jesus.

Since that time, any insincere greeting from someone who has come to betray us or to bring bad news has been called "the kiss of death."

Kissing Someone's Feet

[C] ertain philosophies are expressed in physical terms. For instance, we say, "I'm not going to stand for that," when we disagree with an idea or action. We also say, "I'm not going to take that sitting down."

When the subject turns to feet, it usually has to do with being humbled. Such sayings as "I fell at his feet," with adoration or in forgiveness are usually figurative.

Most of us are repulsed at the thought of kissing someone's feet, literally or figuratively. This expression is usually preceded with a negative qualifying statement such as "I'm not going to . . ." In our society it means paying homage to someone who doesn't deserve it. The thought of it rails against our spirits.

Jesus was the actual recipient of such treatment while he was eating at the home of one of the Pharisees.

"And, behold, a woman in the city, which was a sinner, when she knew that Jesus sat at a meal in the Pharisee's house, brought an alabaster box of ointment. And stood at his feet behind him weeping, and began to wash his feet with tears, and did wipe them with hairs of her head, and kissed his feet, and anointed them with the ointment" (Luke 7:37, 38).

The Pharisee began to grumble and complain that if Jesus were a prophet, he would have known what kind of a woman she was. Jesus, hearing this, told him a story about two debtors who were forgiven of their debts, one of 500 pence and the other of 50 pence. Jesus asked him which debtor would be more grateful. The Pharisee said the one who was relieved of the greater debt.

"Thou gavest me no kiss: but this woman since the time I came in hath not ceased to kiss my feet," Jesus told him (Luke 7:45).

A Labor of Love

John Wesley said that we should do all the good that we can, for as many people as we can, for as long as we can. Helping others without receiving any compensation is known as a "labor of love."

Our efforts might include visiting a sick neighbor, making a meal for a grieving family or doing an errand for someone who is handicapped.

Paul commends the church of Thessalonica in the opening of his first letter to them. He says, "We give thanks to God always for you all, making mention of you in our prayers; Remembering without ceasing your work of faith, and labour of love, and patience of hope in our Lord Jesus Christ, in the sight of God and our Father" (1 Thessalonians 1:2, 3).

The expression a "labor of love," sandwiched between "work of faith" and "patience of hope," has lasted longest in English preference – perhaps because of its alliteration, but also because it joins something that is hard and tough – work – with something that is soft and tender – love.

The world today needs more kind acts than ever before because so many people are hurting. We need to do our Christian deeds without counting the cost or seeking the rewards.

The Land of Nod

To many people, going to the land of Nod means going off to sleep. We use the term "nodding off" to describe people who are no longer able to stay awake, and whose heads begin to nod onto their chests as their eyes blink open and shut.

We may also remember, from our childhood, a poem by Eugene Field about Wynken, Blynken and Nod, who sailed off in a wooden shoe. This bedtime reading is most often associated with sleep.

The land of Nod, however, is a location that is first mentioned in the Bible. It is where Cain went after he had killed his brother, Abel. We read in Genesis 4:16, "And Cain went out from the presence of the Lord, and dwelt in the land of Nod, on the east of Eden."

Nod, while specifically referred to as a real geographic location by the Bible, has become a mystical place to many writers. Cain's place of refuge has also sparked lively discussion about the other residents of Nod. Who were they? Where did they come from?

There has also been a particular fascination with the question, "Whom did Cain marry, if Adam and Eve's family were the only other people on earth?" The logical explanation is that he married one of his sisters.

John Steinbeck took the title for one of his best–selling books, *East of Eden,* from the book of Genesis.

The Last Shall Be First

If you've ever been at the end of a shopping line in a grocery store, you know what a wonderful feeling it is when another cash register opens and you are invited to move from being the last to being the first.

In Matthew 19:27, Peter tells Jesus that he and the other disciples have "forsaken all, and followed Thee." Then he boldly asks what they will receive for making this sacrifice.

Jesus says that when He sits on His throne in Glory the apostles will also sit upon 12 thrones, judging the 12 tribes of Israel. He also says that whatever they have given up in houses, family members or land they will receive a hundredfold in return. He assures them that they will inherit eternal life.

Jesus says, "But many that are first, shall be last; and the last shall be first" (Matthew 19:30).

Jesus follows up His answer by telling the parable of the laborers in the vineyard. In His story, people who are hired last for a farm project are paid first and receive an equal share with those who were hired before them.

God's ways are not our ways. He is far more generous and considerate toward us than we are toward each other. He wants to give us more than we could ever ask or think of asking.

A Law Unto Themselves

Vigilantes are people who take the law into their own hands. They openly attempt to bring about what they see as justice by their own devices. Others who are "a law unto themselves" act in a more covert way. They rationalize their behavior until they think they are above the law, and that it no longer applies to them.

Both are forms of anarchy against an established government. There is another form of willful opposition that is against God's laws. It's called sin.

Paul, the apostle, is referring to the Gentiles when he uses the expression, "a law unto themselves," in the book of Romans.

He says that people who condemn sin in others and commit sins themselves are without excuse, whether they are Jews or Gentiles. In Romans 2:11, he says, "For there is no respect of persons with God."

Paul explains that whether you sin without the law of God or you sin with it, the results are the same – you perish. Then he says, "For when the Gentiles, which have not the law (of God), do by nature the things contained in the law, these, having not the law, are a law unto themselves" (Romans 2:14).

Paul is actually complimenting the Gentiles in Romans 2:14 for behaving according to the law, at times, even though they hadn't formally received God's law. Despite this commendation, the expression, "a law unto themselves," is almost always used in a negative sense today.

To Lead by the Nose

When someone controls another person's actions, we say they are leading that person by the nose. It may be a domineering spouse, a parent, a boss or even a peer. If someone is leading another person by the nose, even figuratively, they are treating him or her the way we would usually expect an animal to be treated. Some animals are led by chains or ropes attached to rings through their noses.

In Isaiah 37:29, we read: "Because thy rage against Me, and thy tumult, is come up into Mine ears, therefore will I put My hook in thy nose, and My bridle in thy lips, and I will turn thee back by the way which thou camest."

This prophecy of God through Isaiah against the nation of Israel came about because the Hebrews were worshipping false gods. God said He would suspend the free–will of the people, and that He would lead them by the nose, as oxen are led. He wanted them to follow Him voluntarily out of love and devotion, but they were selfish and disobedient.

Today, "being led by the nose" is used derisively to describe one who is seen as weak and dehumanized because he has let someone else dominate his life.

Letting Your Hair Down

Being in a relaxed state is sometimes called "letting your hair down." If someone is being too formal or stuffy, friends might tell the person to "chill out" or "let your hair down."

While the saying might suggest the picture of a woman who keeps her hair up most of the time, letting it flow down her back only when she is relaxing – the biblical reference is to a man.

God gave Samson mighty strength as long as he didn't cut his hair, in keeping with a Nazarite vow. It was Delilah who persistently wanted him to tell her his secret as part of a conspiracy to destroy him and his people, the Israelites.

After much nagging and trickery, Samson became vulnerable and relaxed from his vigilance. He told Delilah that the secret of his strength was in a pact he had made with God. Part of his vow was that he wouldn't cut his hair. When Samson finally let down his hair, Delilah cut it off.

We read in Judges 16:19, "and she (Delilah) made him sleep upon her knees; and she called for a man, and she caused him to shave off the seven locks of his (Samson's) head; and she began to afflict him, and his strength went from him."

Letting his hair down in a spiritual matter cost Samson dearly. It proved not only to be dangerous for him and his nation – it actually led to his death.

Like Father, Like Son

Parents get blamed for a lot. Mothers struggle with the tension between home and career, but fathers feel the crunch of criticism, too.

The expression "Like father, like son," has taken on a tone of cynicism in our society. It is akin to saying that one is as bad as the other, although on occasion it is used in a positive sense. Often the tone used, or the circumstances, will indicate whether it's being said as a plus or a minus.

We hear the term "role–model" these days applied to parents. God gave each of us two parents. If we are fortunate enough to have them both available to us during our growing years, we do use them as models. We become somewhat like our parents – for better or for worse.

The Scriptures offer an unusual twist to this familiar saying about parents. The biblical focal point is on the maternal side of the family.

"Behold, everyone that useth proverbs shall use this proverb against thee, saying, As is the mother, so is her daughter" (Ezekiel 16:44).

While children can't be excused for their improper behavior, they do seem to have someone to point a finger toward. The prophet's warning is that others will have the same tendency to blame parents for the way their children act.

How wonderful it is when someone says, "Like father, like son," or "like mother, like daughter," and means it as a compliment.

Like Fuller's Soap

S ome surnames are easily understood. Smith, for instance, relates to a host of professions, such as a silversmith or blacksmith. We may have more difficulty remembering the connection between the name Cooper and barrel–making. Fewer still may recall what a fuller did for a living, even though we may be very familiar with the name Fuller.

Fuller has long been associated with cleaning. Getting things clean is important to most people. Few want to sleep on soiled sheets or drink from unwashed glasses. Some people even insist that the things they own be totally spotless.

God wants purity. He isn't satisfied with half a cleansing. People and the things of God must go through a refining process.

The prophet Malachi, who wrote the last book in the Old Testament, has a message from God on the subject of cleanliness. "But who may abide the day of His coming? and who shall stand when He appeareth? for He is like a refiner's fire and like the fullers' soap" (Malachi 3:2).

A fuller is someone who washes cloth and works to make it white and pure. Mark, referring to Christ's clothing at the Transfiguration says, "And His raiment became shining, exceeding white as snow; so as no fuller on earth can white them" (Mark 9:3).

Like Getting Water from a Rock

S omething that is extremely difficult is said to be "like getting water from a rock." A request for information from a stubborn person, or financial help from someone who is tight with their money, is hard work. The word "squeezing" is sometimes added to this expression – like squeezing water from a rock.

In Numbers 20, Moses is frustrated with the children of Israel. They are in the wilderness, where they spent 40 years wandering in the desert after escaping from slavery. The Hebrew people, whom Moses had led out of captivity through God's power and instruction, had proven to be a complaining lot. They continually claimed that they were better off in Egypt.

The people formed a united front against Moses and Aaron (Numbers 20:2). They rebelled because there was no water to drink.

Moses was frustrated. Instead of waiting for God to supply the water (as He had everything else that they needed), Moses took matters into his own hands.

"And Moses and Aaron gathered the congregation together before the rock, and he said unto them, Hear now ye rebels; must we fetch you water out of this rock? And Moses lifted up his hand, and with his rod he smote the rock twice: and the water came out abundantly, and the congregation drank, and their beasts also" (Numbers 20:10–11).

God had told Moses to gather the people together so that He could satisfy their need for water, but Moses became impatient. In his anger, he didn't wait for God to act. He struck the rock twice and water came from it.

Because of his anger, and his taking credit for getting the water from the rock, God told him that he would not enter into the Promised Land with his people (Numbers 20:12).

Lip Service

A politician, during his first campaign to become president of the United States, made a statement that has become infamous, "Read my lips, no new taxes." Later, he had to take back his promises and the taxes went up. Some people, doubting the sincerity of his pledge, said that he was only paying lip service to get elected.

The expression "lip service" refers to words uttered without sincerity. Politicians are often charged with using lip service to get elected.

Originally, it was God who was receiving the hollow offering of lip service, according to the prophet Isaiah. The Lord revealed to him that the children of Israel were just giving Him empty talk, and that their hearts were not in it.

In Isaiah 29:13 the prophet records, "Wherefore the Lord said, Forasmuch as these people draw near me with their mouth, and with their lips do honour me, but have removed their heart far from me, and their fear toward me is taught by the precept of men." The Lord goes on to say that "the wisdom of their wise men shall perish and the understanding of their prudent men shall be hid" (v. 14).

Empty talk is always dangerous, but especially when directed toward God. People may look on the outward appearance and be fooled, but God looks into our hearts. He knows the level of our sincerity.

A Little Birdie Told Me

A surprised child, punished by her mother for a misdeed that she thought had been kept secret, asked, "How did you know?" Her mother smiled sweetly and said, "A little birdie told me." The child went away deeply confused, but far wiser. Her respect for her mother's knowledge had increased considerably.

Al Capone, the gangster, is reputed to have used this expression, "A little birdie told me," when referring to informers who kept him abreast of his enemies' actions. The phrase "to sing like a bird," which relates to a testimony given by a state's witness, may have some link to this saying.

Solomon originated the phrase when he gave this advice in the Book of Ecclesiastes: "Curse not the king, no not in thy thought; and curse not the rich in thy bedchamber: for a bird of the air shall carry the voice, and that which hath wings shall tell the matter" (Ecclesiastes 10:20).

Solomon was advising against gossip and criticism of people who were in power because of the possible consequences. As a king, he no doubt had many people who came to him with accusations against others in the kingdom. These informers wanted to gain favor with the king. They wanted to turn someone else's misfortune into their own gain.

In the New Testament, James warns, "For every kind of beasts, and of birds, and of serpents, and of things in the sea, is tamed, and hath been tamed of mankind: But the tongue can no man tame; it is an unruly evil, full of deadly poison" (James 3:7, 8).

The Love of Money Is the Root of All Evil

This expression, "The love of money is the root of all evil" has very often been shortened to say that "money is the root of all evil," but money, in and of itself, isn't evil. Our attitude toward money is the corrupting influence.

When we begin to love and cherish money, we lose sight of our priorities. We come into this life without anything material, and we will leave it the same way. A devotion to materialism diminishes our life.

Jesus had an encounter with a rich young ruler who loved possessions so much that he couldn't see that God was more important. He wanted to follow Jesus, as he was invited to, but his love of money caused him to walk away sorrowfully.

This expression is a direct quote from Paul to Timothy in a letter that now comprises a part of the New Testament. "For the love of money is the root of all evil: which while some coveted after, they have erred from the faith, and pierced themselves through with many sorrows" (1 Timothy 6:10).

While the message is 2,000 years old, it is needed in our present generation. Paul's warning to Timothy that many chase after money to their own sorrow is a contemporary truth.

Make Short Work of It

Decision–makers don't waste time. They look at the problem, consider the alternatives and take action. Skilled craftsmen can do a job in half the time it would take someone else, and the finished product will be better. Their ability enables them to make short work of their projects.

Paul the apostle, in the book of Romans, says that God is going to call some people who were not His (chosen) people to be His people. Paul is referring to the Gentiles (Romans 9:25). God had turned Paul's life around on the road to Damascus so that he would be available to minister to the Gentiles.

The further promise for the Gentiles is " . . . that in the place where it was said unto them, (the Gentiles), Ye are not my people; there shall they be called the children of the living God" (Romans 9:26).

In regard to Israel, Paul says that Isaiah prophesied, "Though the number of the children of Israel be as the sand of the sea, a remnant shall be saved: For He (God) will finish the work, and cut it short in righteousness: because a short work will the Lord make upon the earth" (Romans 9:27–28).

God has a plan, and He is working it out in His time.

To Make Someone's Hair Stand on End

A sudden fright gives us goose bumps. It also makes the hair on the back of our necks feel like it is standing out away from our skin. Exaggerated photos of people on posters, who are supposedly frightened, show all of the hair on the person's head standing straight up and out.

When we talk about having a hair–raising experience, we mean that something excited us so much that it felt like our hair stood on end.

Eliphaz, in Old Testament times, had such an experience. His description given in the book of Job may well have contributed to the origin of this expression.

Eliphaz says that something happened to him that made his bones shake (Job 4:14). He says he was in a deep sleep and "Then a spirit [a ghost] passed before my face; the hair of my flesh stood up" (Job 4:15).

This description of fear, trembling and a hair–raising experience made up Eliphaz's personal recollections as he attempted to appeal to Job to make peace with God. He believed Job's afflictions were caused by some secret sin and that they could only be relieved if he would admit to them.

Eliphaz's personal recounting of scary dreams was supposed to motivate Job to take action by asking for forgiveness or mercy from God. Job's hair, however, was lying flat against his head because he felt he had done nothing for which he should be punished.

A Man After His Own Heart

A man who has a similar perspective to another is said to be "a man after his own heart." Saul, the first king of Israel, was a bitter disappointment to his nation and to God. The Philistines were threatening Israel's existence, but Saul was powerless to do anything. He had lost his courage because of his lack of faith in God.

Jonathan, Saul's son, had led a group of Israelites in a sneak attack upon a Philistine garrison. He had been ordered to do so by his father, who refused to seek God's counsel on the matter.

The Philistines sought revenge. Saul, who had nearly disbanded his Army after successfully defeating the Ammonites, was desperate.

Israel was gaining a reputation for being fainthearted, sneaky and cowardly. The people were a disgrace to themselves, and to God. Many were concerned because Samuel, the prophet, was not with Saul in this disturbing hour. They saw Samuel's absence as a sign that God would no longer help Saul, which made them afraid.

Saul waited at Gilgal for seven days for Samuel's arrival, but he didn't come. He then offered a burnt offering, and as soon as the offering had turned to ashes, Samuel came.

Samuel told Saul: "But now thy kingdom shall not continue; the Lord hath sought him a man after his own heart, and the Lord hath commanded him to be captain over his people, because thou hast not kept that which the Lord commanded thee" (1 Samuel 13:14).

The man after God's own heart was David, who succeeded Saul as King of Israel and led his people victoriously over their enemies.

Nail Him to the Wall

S ports commentators use the phrase "nail him" to describe action on a football field or in a hockey arena. Getting "nailed" means getting caught or stopped in some way.

Few people make a connection between the term "nailed" and the crucifixion of Jesus Christ. Nonetheless, his death by being nailed to a cross is one of the most significant events in the history of mankind. Subconsciously, a lot of the "nailing" we do in our expressions relates back to Him, but we lose the connection to Him until we stop and think about it.

The expression, "nail him to the wall," relates to another person in the Bible. He was the first king of the nation of Israel. His name was Saul.

The children of Israel wanted to have a king like all the other countries around them. God was opposed to the idea, but he relented and allowed it. Saul was tall, strong and handsome. He was strong in physical qualities, but he would prove to be very weak in spiritual matters.

Saul became jealous of David, a young man who was eventually going to succeed him as king. He tried to kill David several times, "And Saul cast the javelin: for he said, I will smite David even to the wall with it" (1 Samuel 18:11).

In the end though, it was Saul who got nailed to the wall. He committed suicide by falling on his own sword during the heat of battle. Later his enemies found his body. "And they put his armour in the house of Ashtaroth: and they fastened his body to the wall of Bethshan" (1 Samuel 31:10).

As Old as Methuselah

O nce someone's hair begins to turn gray, people are quick to label them as old. When a person seems especially old, even ancient, some are likely to say the person is "as old as Methuselah."

Methuselah, Noah's grandfather, is the person in the Bible who lived the longest. We read in Genesis 5:27, "And all the days of Methuselah were nine hundred sixty and nine years: and he died."

Methuselah's grandfather, Jared, was the second oldest man who ever lived. He lived to be 962 years old, just seven years short of Methuselah.

Enoch, Methuselah's father, didn't die. He walked with God. According to Genesis 5:24, "And Enoch walked with God: and he was not; for God took him." There is no gravestone or tomb to memorialize him – he went straight to heaven to be with the Lord.

God's original plan for man didn't include death. It came about as a result of Adam and Eve's sin. After the flood, with the exception of Noah, who lived to be 950 years of age, the length of life shortened dramatically. It settled down to a life expectancy of three score and ten (70 years), close to where it is today. Any years beyond 70 are said to be a gift from God and a blessing.

An Old Snake in the Grass

Someone who is sneaky and operates with a hidden agenda is often referred to as "an old snake in the grass." In Genesis 3:1, we read that the serpent was "more subtil than any beast of the field."

Satan, operating as a snake, deceived Eve into disobeying God. He told Eve that she wouldn't die if she disobeyed God, but rather that her eyes would be opened. The serpent said she would be as a god, knowing good from evil.

Because of the snake's deception, Eve ate some of the fruit that God had specifically forbidden her and Adam to eat. They both were tricked into falling from God's grace, bringing terrible consequences for them and the people who came after them.

When God went looking for Adam and Eve, they were hiding. When He asked them why they were hiding, and if they had eaten from the tree that he forbade them, Adam said it was Eve's fault. Eve pointed her finger at the serpent. God then proceeded to curse Satan and to punish the serpent for his actions.

It was indeed the old snake in the grass who had worked his evil through tempting Eve. If you've ever been deceived by someone who appeared to be your friend, but then turned out to be conniving and untrue, you know what motivates people to use this expression to describe them and their slimy behavior.

Out of the Mouths of Babes

God makes strength out of weakness. He often uses the young to confound those who are older. David, who used the expression "out of the mouth of babes" in the Psalms, knew God's ways well.

He was a mere boy when God chose him to be King Saul's successor. It was as a boy that David spoke words of faith and courage. He defeated the giant Goliath, though he was laughed at in the beginning of the battle.

In Psalm 8:1–2, David praises God, saying, "O Lord, our Lord, how excellent is Thy name in all the earth! who has set Thy glory above the heavens. Out of the mouths of babes and sucklings hast Thou ordained strength because of Thine enemies, that Thou mightest still the enemy and the avenger."

Even today, when children speak words that are wise beyond their years, people use this expression to describe their sayings. We sometimes forget that the glory doesn't belong to the child, but to God, who endows whomever He chooses with knowledge and power.

When we train our children in the things of God we will often be surprised by what comes "out of the mouths of babes." The Bible also promises that if we "train up a child in the way he should go . . . when he is old, he will not depart from it." (Proverbs 22:6).

Pass Through the Fire

Major tests or trials are sometimes referred to as "passing through the fire." When we are faced with great difficulties that we would rather avoid, such as illness, grief or other hardships, this expression might apply.

When the children of Israel were held captive by the Assyrians, they adopted many of the strange religious customs of their captors. "And there they burnt incense in all the high places, as did the heathen whom the Lord carried away before them; and wrought wicked things to provoke the Lord to anger" (2 Kings 17:11).

Despite all of God's warnings, they became idol worshippers. They even made their sons and daughters " . . . pass through the fire, and used divination and enchantments, and sold themselves to do evil in the sight of the Lord . . . " (2 Kings 17:17).

The Jews made their children pass through fire (and difficulties) of their own making. God became very angry with them for disobeying His commandment to have no other gods.

When we use this phrase today, it still means going through trials or tribulations. They can either be maladies that befall us, or actions that we bring on ourselves. Whatever their source, enduring them is "passing through the fire."

The Patience of Job

T he virtue of patience has been linked with the name of Job for centuries. This man from the Bible got patience the hard way – he earned it. Job had to endure an enormous number of hardships, including physical torment and the death of loved ones. He also lost all of his possessions, and he had to listen to his friends blame him unjustly for his troubles.

The entire Old Testament book of Job radiates with patience. It is used to overcome countless troubles. After all of his troubles, Job says to the Lord, "I know that Thou canst do every thing, and that no thought can be withholden from Thee" (Job 42:2).

The Bible reminds us that " . . . tribulation worketh patience" (Romans 5:3). A lot of people want patience, but they want it right away. They don't want to have to endure trials and tribulation to get it.

Job endured to the end because he knew he had been faithful to God. He trusted God to restore him, but he resolved to praise God no matter what happened to him.

Job concludes, "Naked came I out of my mother's womb, and naked shall I return thither: the Lord gave, and the Lord hath taken away; blessed be the name of the Lord. In all this Job sinned not, nor charged God foolishly" (Job 1:21, 22).

Peter Out

Fads like video games and Cabbage Patch dolls start out with a great deal of enthusiasm. They are popular for a brief time, until another "in" product hits the market and replaces them.

When something starts off quickly with a lot of energy and then fades or fails, it is said to "Peter out." While the first word of this phrase isn't usually capitalized, I've done so because I believe it refers to the apostle, Peter.

If ever anyone was full of zeal and enthusiasm, it was Peter. He often spoke before he thought, and acted before he considered the outcome.

Whether it was walking on water, asking Jesus if he could build an altar atop the mount of transfiguration or making statements of bravado, Peter always seemed to be first in line. He exuded confidence. He was sure of himself.

Jesus warned him at the Last Supper that he would deny knowing Christ three times before the end of the day. Peter vehemently refuted the warning, saying that he'd be willing to die for Jesus rather than ever denying Him.

Unfortunately for Peter, Christ's words came true. Luke records their face–to–face encounter in the courtyard right after Peter's third denial: "And the Lord turned and looked upon Peter. And Peter remembered the word of the Lord, how He had said unto him, Before the cock crow(s), thou shalt deny me thrice. And Peter went out, and wept bitterly" (Luke 22:61, 62).

Please Don't Babble

I nfants or children who utter gibberish are said to be babbling. We also associate the word "babble" with words not clearly spoken by adults. But how did the word "babble" get into our vocabulary in the first place?

After the great flood, recorded in the book of Genesis, the people embarked on a grand plan to build a city with a tower that would reach up into heaven. Their plan, it seems, was to get closer to God, and to His power.

They wanted to make a name for themselves. They thought they could do it by showing off their great wisdom and their building prowess. Because they all shared the same language, there were no communication barriers. There appeared to be no limit to what they could accomplish.

God wasn't in favor of their plan. He wanted these people, who were dwelling on the Plain of Shinar, to scatter throughout the Earth.

Genesis 11:7 records that the Lord said, "Let us go down, and there confound their language, that they may not understand one another's speech." Their work stopped abruptly because they could no longer communicate.

Verse 9 explains, "Therefore is the name of it (that place) called Babel; because the Lord did there confound the language of all the earth . . . "

The next time you hear someone babbling, remember that it was God who humbled the builders at the Tower of Babel to remind them that He was still in control.

Puffed Up

As children we read about the three little pigs building houses from different types of materials. One used straw, another wood and the third used brick. They were trying to protect themselves from the wicked wolf that was always trying to get them. He had an interesting way of intruding upon them. He would huff and he would puff and then try to blow their houses down. He succeeded with straw and wood, but got stumped by bricks.

We learned early in our lives that things that are puffed up are usually filled with air. They are empty, except for oxygen. Something without substance we say is "filled with hot air."

The word "puff" has a contemporary sound, but it was used in the original translation of the King James Bible in the year 1611.

Paul uses the term "puffed up" six times in his first letter to the church at Corinth. He uses it first to warn against pride (being puffed up) in comparing his work to that of a fellow worker, Apollos (1 Corinthians 4:6).

Being "puffed up" in verses 18 and 19 relates to arrogance regarding their attitude toward his not visiting them soon enough.

Pride is the culprit again in verse 2 of chapter 5, where they are "puffed up" because they haven't mourned over sin among their members.

In 1 Corinthians 8:1, it is knowledge that is "puffed up," while Paul says it is charity (love) that edifies (builds up).

Finally, in the love chapter (13), charity (love) is described as not being "puffed up."

Raising Cain

People who cause a disturbance are sometimes said to be "raising cain." The reference goes back to Adam and Eve's family. Cain was their oldest son. He was a farmer who killed his brother Abel, a shepherd. The murder came about because of jealousy. God had accepted a sacrifice from Abel, but God didn't honor Cain's sacrifice because God saw the evil in his heart (Genesis 4:4–7).

After the murder, Cain told God that he didn't know where his brother was or what had happened to him. He asked God the now infamous question, "Am I my brother's keeper?"

God told Cain, "The voice of thy brother's blood crieth unto Me from the ground" (Genesis 4:10). God then cursed Cain. He told him that the ground would no longer yield crops for him and that he would become a fugitive and a vagabond upon the earth.

Cain pleaded with God for mercy, saying that he would be a hunted man and that people would seek to kill him wherever he went. To protect Cain and to continue his life, God put a mark on him (presumably on his forehead, though the Bible doesn't specifically mention where the mark was made) so that people would not harm him. God said whoever harmed Cain would have vengeance come upon him sevenfold.

By this act, Cain became the first–ever "marked man."

Raising cain nowadays refers to frivolous behavior rather than more serious crimes like murder.

The Root of the Matter

Getting down to the "nitty–gritty" might be a phrase used by country folk, while people in the cities often speak of the "bottom line." Both groups would understand what it means to get to the root of the matter.

A goodly portion of a plant or a tree lies under the surface. We can't see it, but it can be the site of many problems, according to landscapers.

In the Old Testament, Job, in his sorrow and grief, pleads with his friends who have been quick to judge him. He asks them, "Why do you persecute me as God, and are not satisfied with my flesh?" (Job 19:22).

He warns them, "But ye should say, Why persecute we him, seeing the root of the matter (sin) is found in me?" (Job 19:28).

Job tells them, "Be ye afraid of the sword (for yourselves): for wrath bringeth the punishments of the sword, that ye may know there is a judgment" (v. 29).

When we decide to investigate a matter and search out the cause, we must be careful about digging into the root causes of other people's problems. Sometimes we discover our own sin in the problems we see in others.

A Rose Among Thorns

I f a beautiful woman sits between two men, the usual joke is to say that she is "a rose among thorns." Anything or anyone that stands out in comparison to the elements that surround them is likely to be described in this way.

Jesus was known by a host of precious names and titles. One of his titles was the Rose of Sharon. Sharon was an Old Testament city, and an area known for its rich pastures and vegetation.

Another of the word pictures associated with Jesus is the title, "Lily of the Valley." A line from a song says, "He's the Lily of the Valley, He's the bright and morning star . . . "

Solomon draws these floral analogies in a short but pungent book in the Bible known as The Song of Solomon. It is both a poetic and prophetic book that uses a number of symbolic figures for Christ and the Church.

Solomon describes Christ by saying, "I am the rose of Sharon, and the lily of the valleys. As the lily among thorns, so is my love among the daughters" (Song of Solomon 2:1, 2).

The mixing of a rose and a lily in these two verses could account for the rose ending up among the thorns in this expression. At the crucifixion of Jesus, it was the "Rose of Sharon" who wore a crown of thorns. So the true rose among the thorns may well be Christ Himself.

The Salt of the Earth

I f someone says that you are the "salt of the earth," they are paying you a high compliment. Nowadays, people usually say it about older people who have been faithful all of their lives. It is another way of saying that they are solid and dependable.

When people say that someone is an "old salt," they mean that the person is a veteran of many experiences and has proved to be trustworthy.

Jesus told His followers that they were the "salt of the earth" in His Sermon on the Mount. (Matthew 5:13). He warned them, however, that it was possible for salt to lose its flavor and to become useless.

Salt is a preservative. It keeps things from dying. The disciples of Jesus had to remain in Him if they wanted to spread the message of eternal life to others. If they departed from Him, they would lose their spiritual substance and would not be worth their salt.

Jesus continued to encourage his followers in Matthew 5:14 by telling them that they were the light of the world, and that a city set on a hill couldn't be hid. Just as you can taste salt, you can see light.

Christ wanted His disciples to be visible in the world, and to carry with them the savor of His spirit.

A Scapegoat

I n our society, a scapegoat is someone who gets blamed for the misdeeds of others. People in positions of power often try to point the finger at someone else when something goes wrong.

We read in Leviticus 16 about the ritual that was carried out each year on the Day of Atonement. "And Aaron shall lay both his hands upon the head of the live goat, and confess over him all the iniquities of the children of Israel, and all their transgressions in all their sins, putting them upon the head of the goat . . . " (Leviticus 26:21).

The unblemished goat was used symbolically to carry away the sins of the children of Israel. The blood of small animals, brought by each family, was poured onto the back of the goat. The animal was then beaten with a stick until it went off into the wilderness, carrying the sins of the people on its back.

William Tyndale, in 1525, translated a portion of Leviticus 16:26 to read, "To let him go for a scapegoat into the wilderness."

This translation of what might have been called the "escape goat" became accepted and the word scapegoat entered our language.

Scapegoat then began to apply to anyone who was wrongfully accused of something that had been done by someone else. Jesus Christ became the ultimate scapegoat when he died for the sins of the world.

Set Your House in Order

When someone is told to "set their house in order," they aren't being advised on spring cleaning. This expression has become a euphemism that may signal impending death. A doctor, lawyer, minister or a trusted friend may give you this advice so that you can take care of the things that are important to you before you depart this life.

Isaiah gave this advice to King Hezekiah (Isaiah 38:1), who was on his deathbed. The prophet came and told him to set his house in order because God had revealed to Isaiah that Hezekiah would soon die.

Hezekiah, on receiving the news, "turned his face toward the wall, and prayed unto the Lord" (v. 2). In his prayer, he cried to the Lord and reminded Him that he (Hezekiah) had walked in truth and with a perfect heart. He shed many tears and was very sorrowful at the thought of dying.

The Lord heard Hezekiah's prayer and sent Isaiah to give him the good news that the Lord had decided to extend his life. He was told, in Isaiah 38:5, that he would receive an extra 15 years of life because God had heard his prayer and had seen the sincerity of his tears.

No one knows the day or the hour when they will die, but we do know that all of us will, one day, pass from this life to the next. That's why it's important to have our spiritual house in order.

Now the Shoe Is on the Other Foot

T here is a note of "Now you know how it feels" to the expression "Now the shoe is on the other foot." The pain is likened to the discomfort of wearing someone else's shoe or bearing the burden that they formerly had to bear.

In ancient Israel, the taking off of a shoe (sandal) signified the transfer of a contract, or a responsibility. Estates were not transferred in writing, as in modern times, but by a sign. This sign was commonly called "the delivery of seisen." The seisen of a house was signified by the giving of a key, and land was sometimes transferred by the giving of a twig.

In the book of Ruth, Naomi and her daughter-in-law, Ruth, leave Moab and return as poor widows to the land of Judah. Boaz, a prominent and rich relative, befriends them and lets them glean his field. Although another relative is entitled to buy Naomi's field, Boaz reminds him that that if he buys the land he must also marry Ruth and raise a family with her. The kinsman, not wanting to jeopardize his own family's inheritance, relinquishes his rights to Boaz. "Buy it for thee. So he drew off his shoe" (Ruth 4:8).

By taking off his shoe, this man made a public declaration that he was surrendering a valuable parcel of land. He was, however, also transferring a responsibility that he did not want to assume. Now the shoe was on the other foot (Boaz's), but he was happy to wear it because he loved Ruth. The land was a bonus.

Sour Grapes

Blaming someone else for our misfortune or lack of success is usually seen as a weak excuse. Calling such an attitude "sour grapes" goes back a very long way.

In the Bible, we read a lot about children suffering because of the sins of their parents. The prophets of old spent a lot of their time chastising these parents, particularly the fathers, for their behavior. They warned them that they would be punished for the grief that they had caused their children.

In Ezekiel 18:2, 3 God speaks out against this ancient parable of sour grapes, "What mean ye, that ye use this proverb concerning the land of Israel, saying, The fathers have eaten sour grapes, and the children's teeth are set on edge? As I live, saith the Lord God, ye shall not have occasion any more to use this proverb in Israel."

God is saying, through Ezekiel, that the people of Israel have no more excuses. The parents aren't completely off the hook; they are still responsible for their sins. The reason the proverb should be put away is that the children are each accountable for the sins they commit. They can't just keep on blaming their parents for the way they are with a sour grapes attitude.

The next time you are tempted to blame someone else for what's happening to you, be careful because it may be "sour grapes" on your part.

Spare the Rod and Spoil the Child

In a permissive age, this biblical adage has come under a lot of fire. It has been deemed as controversial, and possibly abusive advice.

While some have used this advice as license to bully their children, many people have dismissed its wisdom without consideration. Most people say that they don't want to have "spoiled children." They are not always sure how to avoid such an outcome.

Solomon says in Proverbs 13:24, "He that spareth his rod hateth his son: but he that loveth him chasteneth him betimes."

The wisdom of the original admonishment is even stronger than the current form of this expression. It suggests that if you hold back from correcting your child, then you don't love him or her enough.

In Hebrews 12:6, it says, "Whom the Lord (God) loveth he chasteneth . . . " Paul says that God corrects us not because he hates us, but because he loves us and he wants the best for us. Verse 7 of Hebrews 12 concludes . . . "for what son is he whom the father chasteneth not."

Discipline takes time and energy and shows deep concern. Remember, Solomon says you "chasten betimes" (at the appropriate time), not continuously, which amounts to abuse.

Sparks Are Flying

Friction causes sparks to fly. A few minutes of observation in a foundry will prove that to be true. When we use this expression, we usually are referring to friction between human beings. If someone is having an argument that becomes heated we might say, "sparks are flying."

While we may think of sparks as a fairly modern word, this expression is recorded in what some theologians consider to be the oldest book in the Bible. Job is receiving advice during his troubles from a man named Eliphaz the Temanite. He is telling Job, "Man is born unto trouble, as the sparks fly upward" (Job 5:7).

Since the inception of this quote, "trouble" and "sparks flying" seem to have gone hand–in–hand. A contemporary gospel song reminds us, "It only takes a spark to get a fire going." That reference is a positive one. It speaks of God's love. Most people, however, still think cautiously about sparks because they fear that sparks will lead to a raging fire.

For that reason, the general rule of thumb has been to avoid conflicts. People may be curious and remain briefly during the start of an argument, but most usually walk away as soon as it becomes heated – when the sparks start flying.

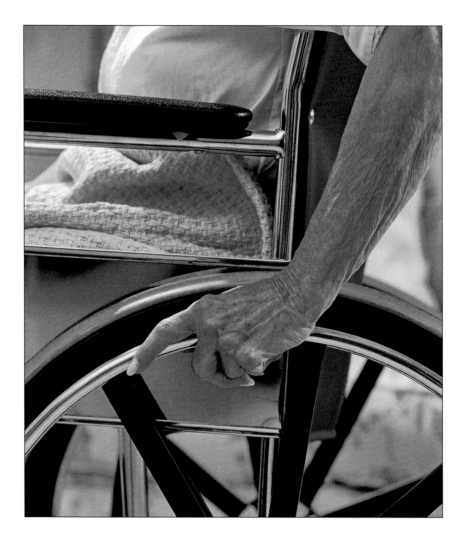

The Spirit Is Willing, But The Flesh Is Weak

As people get older they say things like "the spirit is willing, but the flesh is weak," to let others know they are getting tired. It's another way of saying they have a desire to do things and to go places, but they don't have the energy.

Others, far younger, sometimes say, "the spirit is willing, but the flesh is weak," as an excuse to indulge in activities that they know might be morally questionable.

Few people who use this common expression would attribute it to Jesus. He said it to some of His disciples in the Garden of Gethsemane, just before He was arrested prior to His Crucifixion.

He had gone to the garden to pray. He told most of His disciples to sit in one place while he went further into the garden with Peter, James, and John. He told these three, "My soul is exceeding sorrowful, even unto death: tarry ye here, and watch with Me" (Matthew 26:38).

Jesus went a little further away from them and fell on His face and prayed to His heavenly Father, asking that the cup of death might be taken away from Him. But He also declared His willingness to drink from the cup if there was no other way to fulfill the purpose for which He had come to earth – the salvation of mankind.

After Christ prayed this prayer, He returned to Peter, James, and John. He found them asleep, and He woke Peter and said, " . . . What, could ye not watch with Me one hour? Watch and pray, that ye enter not into temptation: the spirit indeed is willing, but the flesh is weak" (Matthew 26:40, 41).

Staying alert to spiritual matters is essential to the Christian life. If we aren't diligent, we will become weary in our well doing.

A Stone's Throw Away

Any short distance that can be easily reached is sometimes referred to as being "a stone's throw away." This expression, not to be taken literally, means that something is close by. Nowadays we might say, "It's in the neighborhood."

"A stone's throw" is the distance that Luke's Gospel says Jesus was from His disciples as He prayed in the Garden of Gethsemane prior to being betrayed by Judas.

Luke relates that Jesus came often to this garden to pray. He may very well have had a particular spot in the garden that He preferred. His disciples were familiar with His habits – they knew that He often drew away by Himself to pray. The Gospel writers make several references to this discipline. They also say that most often He went off to a "lonely" place or a "deserted" place.

Immediately following the Last Supper with His disciples, " . . . He came out, and went, as He was wont, to the Mount of Olives; and His disciples also followed Him. And when He was at the place, He said unto them, Pray that ye enter not into temptation. And He was withdrawn from them about a stone's cast, and kneeled down and prayed" (Luke 22:39–41).

While the disciples were only a stone's throw away from Him physically, they were a million miles away from His agony. They fell asleep while Jesus prayed.

Straight and Narrow

During the 1970s the words "straight" and "narrow" both came under fire in our secular society. To a generation that was saying, "do your own thing" and "anything goes," any restricting words were unwelcome.

For many generations, "walking the straight and narrow pathway" was to be commended. The phrase of praise, "straight as an arrow," may have been a variation on the original saying. Additionally, an arrow must fly straight to hit its target.

If some are walking on the straight and narrow pathway, then it must be assumed there are other roads to choose from as well. The Bible says these other roads lead to destruction, but they are crowded nonetheless.

Jesus advises, "Enter ye in at the strait gate: for wide is the gate, and broad is the way, that leadeth to destruction, and many there be which go in thereat: Because strait is the gate and narrow is the way, which leadeth unto life, and few there be that find it" (Matthew 7:13–14). The word strait in this translation means narrow as well.

In John 14:6, Jesus says that He is the Way, the Truth and the Life and that no man comes to God except through Him.

That's pretty straight.

Strain at a Gnat and Swallow a Camel

Some people love to major in minors. They magnify tiny things that they think are significant, while things of significance get past them on a regular basis. In a financial sense, they're the folks who are "penny wise and pound foolish."

At the close of His earthly ministry, Jesus directs this barb about a gnat and a camel at the religious leaders of the day. He refers to the scribes and Pharisees as hypocrites. He says that they pay their tithe of mint and anise and cummin to the temple, but they have omitted the weightier matters of the law such as judgment, mercy and faith. Jesus tells them that they haven't done what they should have, and that they should have left undone what they did do (Matthew 23:23).

Christ chastises them, "Ye blind guides, which strain at a gnat, and swallow a camel" (v. 24).

He tells them that they willingly clean the outside of a cup and platter, but that within they are full of extortion and excess (v. 25).

Jesus used these extremely vivid word pictures and stories so that his hearers would recall the lessons that he taught them. One of his other lessons had to do with a camel going through the eye of a needle.

A Stumbling Block

Most of us want to be thought of as building blocks, or at least as stepping–stones for others. Sometimes, in spite of our best intentions, we become a stumbling block for someone else.

There are several references to "stumbling blocks," or "stones of stumbling," in the Bible. Usually these stumbling blocks are sins that have caused others to fall.

The Christians in Rome received the following good advice from the Apostle Paul, "Let us not therefore judge one another any more: but judge this rather, that no man put a stumbling block or an occasion to fall in his brother's way" (Romans 14:13).

Paul was concerned that he might be causing offense to young Christians by something he was doing. He was purchasing meat that had been used as an offering to idols, and then was later sold. Many people took advantage of these sales because it was the finest meat available at a reasonable price.

Some Christians found the practice offensive. Paul said that idols meant nothing to him, and so any such offerings were meaningless. He wanted to be careful, however, not to cause someone else difficulty because of his behavior.

He says to others who have purchased the meat, "But take heed lest by any means this liberty of yours become a stumbling block to them that are weak" (1 Corinthians 8:9).

Paul concludes, in 1 Corinthians 8:13, that he would never want to do anything that might cause another to fall spiritually, even if it meant sacrifice on his part to keep from being a stumbling block to someone else.

The Tables Are Turned

T here is an implied note of revenge in this expression. You can almost hear the sound "Aha" or the words, "at last" which might precede the phrase, "Now the tables are turned." "Getting even" seems to be a much sought after feeling. People have often cried in vain, "Is there no justice?"

The money changers in the temple at Jerusalem had long been robbing the people by charging them improperly when they had to exchange other currencies for temple money.

Jesus became enraged at seeing this. The menagerie of sacrificial animals and other items being sold within the temple entrance also disturbed him.

"And they (the disciples) come to Jerusalem: and Jesus went into the temple, and began to cast out them that sold and bought in the temple, and overthrew the tables of the money changers, and the seats of them that sold doves" (Mark 11:15).

The people were powerless, but Jesus turned the tables on those who were cheating the people. He also cleansed the temple of those who had forgotten that it was supposed to be a house of prayer.

To Take Under Your Wing

Protection and concern are the main themes of this common saying, "To take under your wings." A schoolteacher or a camp counselor is sometimes encouraged to show special attention to a young person who has particular needs. This special care is sometimes described as "hovering wings."

In business, when an experienced worker shows interest in the career of someone less experienced, he is said to be "taking him under his wing."

This word picture of warmth and safety is accompanied by practical concern and instruction. In Psalm 63:7, David refers to God's care for him when he says, "because Thou has been my help, therefore in the shadow of Thy wings will I rejoice."

David recognized that having God as his caregiver was a great reason to rejoice. Too often people are reluctant to give themselves over to God's care and protection.

In the last week before His Crucifixion, Jesus addressed the multitudes gathered in the temple in Jerusalem. He said, "O Jerusalem, Jerusalem, thou that killest the prophets, and stonest them which are sent unto thee, how often would I have gathered thy children together, even as a hen gathered her chicks under her wings and ye would not?" (Matthew 23:37).

The people of Jerusalem rejected Jesus, though He longed to embrace them. He wanted to take them under His wing, but instead they shouted, "Crucify Him, crucify Him."

Teeth Set on Edge

I f something bothers our minds, it will also affect our bodies. Anxiety will cause us to perspire, it may dilate our eyes or even set our teeth on edge. This may be where the term "to be on edge" began.

Certain foods can also set our teeth on edge. If what we eat is extreme in temperature, our teeth are sensitized. Foods that have a peculiar tartness can also cause our mouth to react.

Jeremiah, the prophet, is bringing a message of hope concerning the coming of Christ. He speaks of God building and planting anew. The fruit that is to come, according to Jeremiah's message from the Lord, is good fruit.

Thus we read, "In those days they shall say no more, The fathers have eaten a sour grape, and the children's teeth are set on edge" (Jeremiah 31:29).

The prophet warns parents not to continue in sin because their children, and future generations, will be affected by their iniquities. There are many references to the sins of parents being "visited" upon their children in the Old Testament, particularly in the Torah (the first five books of the Bible).

There's Nothing New Under the Sun

"**S**ame old thing," children are often heard to say. They seem to have an endless need for adventure, and especially for new things to stimulate their thinking. Solomon wasn't a child when he said, "There's nothing new under the sun." In fact, he was a king – the King of Israel. He was reputed to be one of the wealthiest, most educated and one of the best men who ever lived.

It isn't just boredom that causes him to utter this expression. He isn't just childishly chanting, "There's nothing new – there's nothing to do."

He is laying his soul bare before us in the book of Ecclesiastes. He is wrestling with the meaning of life. He refers to life as "chasing the wind."

In the first chapter of Ecclesiastes, he recites a litany of disappointments which we still hear today: "All is vanity" (v. 2); "The sun also ariseth (rises), and the sun goeth (goes) down" (v. 5); "All the rivers run into the sea, yet the sea is not full" (v. 7).

Solomon says, "The thing that hath been it is that which shall be; and that which is done is that which shall be done: and there is no new thing under the sun" (1:9).

While Solomon repeats variations of this phrase often in his book of Ecclesiastes, he does, in the end, come to a resolve. "Let us hear the conclusion of the whole matter: Fear God, and keep His commandments: for this is the whole duty of man" (12:13).

A Thorn in Your Side

When a problem won't go away, we call it a thorn in our side. It can be a nagging, persistently annoying person or circumstance for which we seem to have no solution. The children of Israel, by disobeying God, inherited thorns that wouldn't leave them for generations to come.

In Judges 2:3, an angel of God delivers the message that, because the Israelites had formed allegiances with idol–worshipping nations against the commands of God, those nations shall now be " . . . as thorns in your sides, and their gods shall be a snare unto you."

Sometimes we are our own worst enemies. Our selfish, sinful natures cause us to disobey God, and then we must suffer the consequences.

Despite several warnings from God about the dangers and effects of idolatry, Israel couldn't seem to avoid the temptation. "Thorns" plagued the total conquest of the Promised Land, which God had covenanted to them, because the Jews collaborated and cohabited with their enemies.

Paul, in 2 Corinthians 12:7, speaks of a "thorn in the flesh," which he says was given to him as a "messenger of Satan" to buffet him, lest he be exalted above measure.

Sometimes, a thorn in our side is used to humble us.

Three Score and Ten

Abraham Lincoln, speaking at Gettysburg, opened his remarks with a biblical sounding phrase, "Four score and seven years ago." A score is 20, so he was talking about something that happened 87 years before his speech.

When the Bible speaks of three score and ten, it is talking about a period of 70 years. This period of time became the normal number of years that a person could expect to live, according to several scriptural references.

People lived very long lives in the early days of mankind. It was because God's original plan was that man wouldn't die. Sin brought death, and following the great flood, life spans became much shorter.

After Moses, who lived to be 120 years old, we begin to see people normally living to about 70, close to the life expectancy today in most developed nations.

In Psalm 90, a prayer of Moses is recorded in which he defines the normal length of life. "The days of our years are threescore and ten; and if by reason of strength they be fourscore years, yet is their strength, labour and sorrow; for it is soon cut off and we fly away" (Psalm 90:10).

To fly away is to die, and hopefully to wing our way toward heaven.

To a 'T'

"**W**ell, that just suits me to a 'T'," the little red–haired girl said with indignation when her friend told her that she wouldn't play with her "ever again."

Many of us have used this expression at some point in our lives. Few people have ever stopped to think about how it got into our language.

It originated with Hebrew scribes, who did much of their writing with tiny brushes. Several of the letters in their alphabet looked alike and could only be properly identified by the position of the little brush marks that accompanied each letter. These marks were called "horns." Expert scribes prided themselves on getting every letter exactly right or "to a horn."

In Wycliffe's English translation of the Bible (1382), he made reference to the horn, calling it a "titil." The verse he translated was Matthew 5:18, "for verily I say unto you, till heaven and earth pass, one jot or one tittle shall in no wise pass from the law till all be fulfilled."

"Titil" became tittle, but a proverbial expression in the meantime was born – "To a T." It is used to speak of perfection and as a sign of pleasure with one's work or situation.

Turning the Other Cheek

G handi provided a contemporary example for Martin Luther King, Jr., when he was looking for a model of nonviolence. Dr. King had heard about Jesus since he was a child, so the philosophy of Christ was real to him. He knew that Jesus practiced nonviolence, and he was encouraged in reading about Ghandi to see that these principles, put into action, could change a nation.

He had a hard time convincing people in the civil rights movement that "turning the other cheek" would work. His efforts and the courage of countless others proved convincingly that what Jesus taught was true.

Christ gave this spiritual advice, which our human nature has a hard time accepting. "But, I say unto you, which hear, Love your enemies, do good to them which hate you, Bless them that curse you, and pray for them which despitefully use you. And unto him that smiteth thee on the one cheek offer also the other . . ." (Luke 6:27–29).

In the Gospel of Matthew this exhortation is linked with Jesus refuting the Old Testament teaching on retaliation (Matthew 5:38, 39).

This teaching reinforces the Biblical principle that God's ways are not our ways – they are above our natural inclinations. We could change our world for good, if we were only brave enough to practice what Jesus preached.

Turn the World Upside Down

The movie, The Poseidon Adventure, tells the fictional story of an ocean liner that is turned upside down by an underwater earthquake. The ship's surviving passengers then encounter a series of problems as they seek to find their way to the bottom of the ship, which of course is now the top. Their ship was named after the mythical Greek god Poseidon, who was the god of waters, earthquakes, and horses.

People going through emotional or physical upsets often talk about "their world being turned upside down." It seems to be used a lot when families are moving from one house to another.

This colorful phrase was used to refer to the disciples of Jesus in the book of Acts. Paul and Silas had just concluded an evangelistic crusade at a synagogue in Thessalonica. They preached Christ, and many people were accepting Him as their Savior.

They won over many converts, including "a great multitude (of Greeks)" and more than a few of the "chief women" (Acts 17:4). Their success led to envy among non-believing Jews and prompted a riot.

"But the Jews which believed not, moved with envy, took unto them certain lewd fellows of the baser sort, and gathered a company, and set all the city on an uproar, and assaulted the house of Jason, and sought to bring them out to the people. And when they found them not, they drew Jason and certain brethren unto the rulers of the city, crying, These that have turned the world upside down are come hither also" (Acts 17: 5–6).

Two Heads Are Better Than One

The statement, "two heads are better than one," which relates to cooperation and working together, has remained constant in its intent since it was written nearly 3,000 years ago (935 BC). It comes from a portion of Scripture in the book of Ecclesiastes.

Solomon, the writer, is speaking of vanity. He says that it is vain to work alone because there is no end to one's labor and no one to carry it on. Vanity, as he uses it, is not foolish pride, but rather emptiness or futility.

There is a profound note of sadness in his observations. Solomon, the powerful king, was lonely and depressed. He thought that life was like chasing the wind.

He asks in Ecclesiastes 4:8, "For whom do I labour, and bereave my soul of good? This is also vanity, yea, it is a sore travail."

Solomon then takes heart and declares in the ninth and tenth verses: "Two are better than one; because they have a good reward for their labour. For if they fall, the one will lift up his fellow: but woe to him that is alone when he falleth; for he hath not another to help him up."

John Heywood added the words "heads" to the proverb in 1546 when he wrote, "two heddis are better than one head."

In Brewer's Dictionary of Phrase and Fable a question is added to the phrase: "Two heads are better than one, or why do folks marry?"

God has made us to love Him and to love each other. He wants us to work together in peace and harmony. Doing our "own thing" can isolate us and leave us unfulfilled. Sharing our hopes and dreams as we work together gives our lives purpose and meaning.

Wash Your Hands of a Matter

When we want to be finished with something that is unpleasant, we say that "we have washed our hands of the matter." We also say that it is "over and done with."

Somehow people believe that they can use these expressions to bring matters to a close. They also seem to think that from the moment they say them, they are free from any further responsibility.

The person who originally made this phrase famous believed he was doing exactly that. But 2,000 years later, no one seems fooled by his declaration.

Pontius Pilate was the governor that Jesus came to after he was arrested in the Garden of Gethsemane. As a Roman, Pilate wasn't really interested in what he considered religious squabbles among the Jews. He would have been much happier if he had never had to deal with them.

After talking to Jesus, he was convinced that He was innocent of all charges. He tried to escape having to make a decision about releasing Jesus. He proposed to the people that Jesus be the person whom the governor could set free, if they agreed. But the people had been stirred up to reject this idea. They yelled, "Crucify him! Crucify him!"

"When Pilate saw that he could prevail nothing, but that rather a tumult was made, he took water, and washed his hands before the multitude, saying I am innocent of the blood of this just person, see ye to it" (Matthew 27:24).

A Wolf in Sheep's Clothing

A wolf cannot be trusted. Every child who watches cartoons on TV on Saturday mornings knows that. The wolf is always the villain. He often dresses up in disguises to look like something other than a wolf. He has even been known to don a sheepskin to try to fool the flock.

The expression, "A wolf in sheep's clothing," seems to have originated with Aesop, who wrote a book of fables hundreds of years before Christ came to earth.

Jesus uses a similar analogy to describe false prophets. Jesus warns, "Beware of false prophets, which come to you in sheep's clothing, but inwardly they are ravening wolves. Ye shall know them by their fruits" (Matthew 7:15, 16).

He goes on to say that only good plants can produce good fruit, but that corrupt trees will always produce bad fruit. Trees that don't produce good fruit are only good enough to be burned in the fire.

The Bible has often taught that outward appearances can be deceiving, but that God looks on the heart. We can't look into a person's heart, but we are able to see the spiritual fruit that they produce, or fail to produce.

Don't be quick to judge, but be discerning. You will know the wolf by his behavior, and you won't be fooled.

Crest $ *Books*

Salvation Army National Publications

Crest Books, a division of The Salvation Army's National Publications department, was established in 1997 so contemporary Salvationist voices could be captured and bound in enduring form for future generations, to serve as witnesses to the continuing force and mission of the Army.

Shaw Clifton, *Never the Same Again: Encouragement for new and not–so–new Christians,* 1997

Compilation, *Christmas Through the Years: A War Cry Treasury*, 1997

William Francis, *Celebrate the Feasts of the Lord: The Christian Heritage of the Sacred Jewish Festivals*, 1998

Marlene Chase, *Pictures from the Word,* 1998

Joe Noland, *A Little Greatness*, 1998

Lyell M. Rader, *Romance & Dynamite: Essays on Science & the Nature of Faith,* 1998

Shaw Clifton, *Who Are These Salvationists? An Analysis for the 21st Century*, 1999

Compilation, *Easter Through the Years: A War Cry Treasury*, 1999

Terry Camsey, *Slightly Off Center! Growth Principles to Thaw Frozen Paradigms*, 2000

Philip Needham, *He Who Laughed First: Delighting in a Holy God*, (in collaboration with Beacon Hill Press, Kansas City), 2000

Henry Gariepy, ed., *A Salvationist Treasury: 365 Devotional Meditations from the Classics to the Contemporary*, 2000

Marlene Chase, *Our God Comes: And Will Not Be Silent*, 2001

A. Kenneth Wilson, *Fractured Parables: And Other Tales to Lighten the Heart and Quicken the Spirit*, 2001

Carroll Ferguson Hunt, *If Two Shall Agree* (in collaboration with Beacon Hill Press, Kansas City), 2001

John C. Izzard, *Pen of Flame: The Life and Poetry of Catherine Baird*, 2002

Henry Gariepy, *Andy Miller: A Legend and a Legacy*, 2002

Compilation, *A Word in Season: A Collection of Short Stories,* 2002

R. David Rightmire, S*anctified Sanity: The Life and Teaching of Samuel Logan Brengle*, 2003

Chick Yuill, *Leadership on the Axis of Change,* 2003

Compilation, *Living Portraits Speaking Still: A Collection of Bible Studies,* 2004

A. Kenneth Wilson, T*he First Dysfunctional Family: A Modern Guide to the Book of Genesis,* 2004

Allen Satterlee, *Turning Points: How The Salvation Army Found a Different Path,* 2004

David Laeger, Shadow and Substance: T*he Tabernacle of the Human Heart*, 2005

Check Yee, *Good Morning China,* 2005

Marlene Chase, *Beside Still Waters: Great Prayers of the Bible for Today*, 2005

Roger J. Green, *The Life & Ministry of William Booth* (in collaboration with Abingdon Press, Nashville), 2006

Norman H. Murdoch, *Soldiers of the Cross: Susie Swift and David Lamb*, 2006

Henry Gariepy, *Israel L. Gaither: Man with a Mission*, 2006

R.G. Moyles (ed.), I *Knew William Booth,* 2007

John Larsson, *Saying Yes to Life*, 2007

Frank Duracher, *Smoky Mountain High,* 2007

R.G. Moyles, *Come Join Our Army*, 2008

Ken Elliott, *The Girl Who Invaded America: The Odyssey Of Eliza Shirley*, 2008

Notes

Notes

Notes

Notes

Notes